JURASSIC PARK™
INSTITUTE

Dinosaur Field Guide

by
Dr. Thomas R. Holtz, Jr.
and
Dr. Michael Brett-Surman

illustrated by
Robert Walters

Proceed with caution!

Random House New York

Special thanks to the following people for their work on this book:

At Random House:

Jason Zamajtuk, Assistant Art Director

Alice Jonaitis, Senior Editor

Alice Alfonsi, Editorial Director

Artie Bennett, Copy Chief

Jenny Golub, Christopher Shea, Colleen Fellingham, Copyeditors

Fred Pagan, Production Manager

Lisa Findlay, Editorial Assistant

Jonathan Ellis, Design Assistant

Andrew Barthelmes, Design Assistant

At Universal Studios:

Cindy Chang, Executive Editor

Library of Congress Cataloging-in-Publication Data
Holtz, Thomas R., 1965– Jurassic Park Institute dinosaur field guide / by Thomas R. Holtz, Jr. and Michael Brett-Surman ; illustrated by Robert Walters ; with photographs from the Jurassic Park films.
   p. cm.
ISBN 0-375-81293-8
1. Dinosaurs—Encyclopedias, Juvenile. 2. Jurassic Park (Motion Picture)—Encyclopedias, Juvenile. [1. Dinosaurs.]
I. Title: Dinosaur field guide. II. Brett-Surman, M. K., 1950– III. Walters, Robert, ill. IV. Title.   QE861 .3 .H65 2001   567.9—dc21   2001019536

www.randomhouse.com/kids

www.jpinstitute.com

First Edition

Printed in the United States of America   June 2001   10 9 8 7 6 5 4 3 2 1

Contents

WHY ARE DINOSAURS SO POPULAR?

Hollywood has been featuring dinosaur-inspired creatures in movies for years, from the many versions of Sir Arthur Conan Doyle's The Lost World to The Beast from 20,000 Fathoms, Godzilla, and Jurassic Park. What could be more exciting than seeing such amazing creatures on the big screen? Yet Hollywood is not the only reason that dinosaurs are so popular.

The award-winning book The Complete Dinosaur suggests dinosaurs are popular because they represent "adventure, power, time travel, science, mystery, [and] lost worlds." But what truly sets dinosaurs apart from other popular movie creatures is that dinosaurs were REAL. They were not part of some backdrop; they actually ruled our world for more than 140 million years—that's 75 times longer than our own human species! Even though many dinosaur movies are loaded with inaccuracies (they are, after all, not documentaries, but entertainment!), they often spark our desire to know more. And that's why we've written this book: to tell you more about these amazingly popular creatures.

There are now over 850 members of the group Dinosauria and the number grows by about 10 each year! So how did we narrow that 850 down to the 100 entries in this book? We wanted to give you a sample from every dinosaur group, and to include several that are familiar—some that have been around since being discovered in the 1800s, some featured in the Jurassic Park movies, several that were named during our lifetime, and some brand-new ones.

Since the "Dinosaur Renaissance" began in 1975, the number of professional dinosaur paleontologists (people who work on dinosaurs full-time at the professional level) has risen from about 20 to over 100. This has led to an explosion of new explorations and discoveries. At one time, North America was the center for new finds. Now China and Argentina lead the world in finding and naming new dinosaur species. With about 10 new species named per year, scientists learn something new about dinosaurs literally each month. The field of vertebrate paleontology is one of the most interdisciplinary of the sciences. Each year it will see new growth, new students, and new adventures. Care to join us?

Finally, there is one dark side to the sometimes "overpopularity" of dinosaurs. They now have a commercial value that makes the unethical and illegal collecting of fossils financially rewarding in some cases. For every dinosaur fossil with scientific value that gets collected as a "trophy," or winds up in a "non-permanent" collection, the whole world and all future citizens run the risk of losing the equivalent of a page of Shakespeare. In the words of fictional character Indiana Jones (regrettably an archaeologist—not a paleontologist), "It belongs in a museum."

When Was the Age of Dinosaurs?

The Age of Dinosaurs began about 250 million years ago (mya), during a time known as the Mesozoic Era. Now, to us humans, who have only been around for about 1.5 million years, 250 million years may seem like a long time ago. But it really isn't that long when you consider it as a part of what scientists call Geologic Time, or the time measured from today back to the birth of Earth—about 4.5 billion years!

The first eight–ninths of Earth's history, from 4.5 billion to 544 million years ago, are called Precambrian (pree-CAIM-bree-in) Time. The oldest fossils show up in the early Precambrian about 3.75 billion years ago. These earliest fossils were of bacteria, the simplest known living things. More complex fossils, including traces of worm-like animals, show up much later in Precambrian Time. Because early life did not have hard parts, the fossil record is very sparse in the Precambrian. However, at around 544 million years ago animals developed shells, bones, teeth, and other hard parts. From this time onward, fossils become common. Scientists refer to the time from 544 million years ago to today as the Phanerozoic (FAN-uh-ro-ZO-ick), or "visible life," Eon. This eon is divided into three eras.

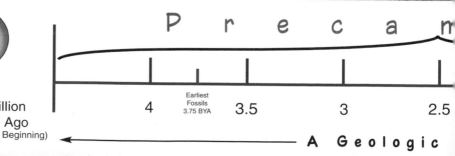

P r e c a m

4.5 Billion Years Ago
(Earth's Beginning)

4   Earliest Fossils 3.75 BYA   3.5   3   2.5

A Geologic

PALEOZOIC ERA

The first era of visible life is called the Paleozoic (PAY-lee-o-ZO-ick), or "ancient life," Era. This is when trilobites (an extinct group of sea-dwelling relatives of insects, crustaceans, and spiders) lived, fishes ruled the seas, and the first plants, insects, and amphibians (animals with backbones that live on land but must be in water to reproduce) colonized the land. It was late in the Paleozoic that descendants of the amphibians developed shelled eggs, evolved, and split into the two major groups of dominant land vertebrates (backboned animals) that have ruled until today. One group is called the synapsids, which includes the mammals (humans among them) and our protomammal ancestors. The other, and far larger, group is called the reptiles. Reptiles include turtles, lizards and snakes, crocodilians, dinosaurs, and various other extinct groups.

During the Paleozoic a series of collisions between continents produced the supercontinent of Pangaea (pan-JEE-a), which means "all Earth." Pangaea was mostly in the Southern Hemisphere. All of Earth's landmasses were pushed together, surrounded by a single ocean—Panthalassa (pan-tha-LAS-a), or "all sea." The Paleozoic Era ended with the most sweeping extinction known in Earth's history, which may have been caused by the biggest series of volcanic eruptions in the Phanerozoic Eon, the remains of which are found in Siberia. It is estimated that more than 95 percent of all animal species went extinct.

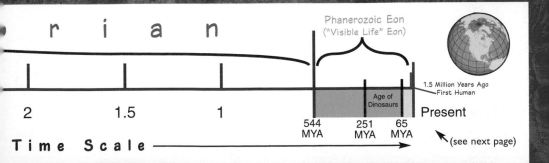

r i a n

Phanerozoic Eon
("Visible Life" Eon)

1.5 Million Years Ago
First Human

2   1.5   1   544   251   65   Present
                                   MYA   MYA   MYA

Age of
Dinosaurs

T i m e   S c a l e

(see next page)

MESOZOIC ERA

The second era of the Phanerozoic Eon was the Mesozoic (MES-o-ZO-ick) Era, or Age of Dinosaurs. The supercontinent of Pangaea began to break apart and a new ocean formed in the split between North America and Africa. This new area became the Atlantic Ocean. Many continents started to drift northward. North America traveled across the equator into its current position. It was possible to walk from New York to London. South America began to separate from Africa. Antarctica was still connected to Australia and India.

(1) Triassic Period

The first of the three geologic periods within the Mesozoic is the Triassic (trie-AS-ick). This was a very interesting time. At its beginning, most of the ecologically dominant synapsids (protomammals) were replaced by reptiles. Dinosaurs, winged pterosaurs, crocodilians, lizards, and turtles all first appeared during the Late Triassic, as did the first mammals.

(2) Jurassic Period

The second period of the Mesozoic is called the Jurassic (joo-RAS-ick). This was the "age of giants." Sauropods, or long-necked plant-eaters, became the largest land animals of all time. Theropods, or meat-eaters, became the most diverse (having the largest number of species) group of land predators, and the first birds appeared from one of these theropod groups. Ornithischians (the main group of plant-eating dinosaurs) were mostly represented by the armored ankylosaurs and the plated stegosaurs.

(3) Cretaceous Period

The third, longest, and final period of the Mesozoic is called the Cretaceous (kri-TAY-shus). Sauropod species declined in the Northern Hemisphere but flourished in the Southern Hemisphere—especially the titanosaurs. Theropods experienced their greatest diversity of groups, from tyrannosaurs to birds. The bird groups expanded and diversified into the seabirds, predators, waterfowl, and the flightless runners and swimmers. The plated dinosaurs went extinct, but the armored dinosaurs split into three groups. Ornithopods (two-legged herbivores) also diversified and finally resulted in the most elegant of dinosaurs (the duckbills with their crests) and the most elaborate dinosaurs (the ceratopsians with their frills of bone up to 10 feet/3 m long). The final group of dinosaurs also appeared: the pachycephalosaurs, or boneheads. As far as we can tell from the fossil record, the largest number of dinosaur species occurred at this time. Then it all ended about 65 million years ago in the fourth-largest extinction event in Earth's history. (The three larger extinction events were in the Paleozoic Era.)

Phanerozoic Eon

Paleozoic		Mesozoic (The Age of Dinosaurs)			Cenozoic
		Triassic	Jurassic	Cretaceous	

544 MYA   251 MYA   65 MYA   Present

The reasons for the extinction of the Mesozoic dinosaurs (excluding birds) are very complex and still debated by scientists. Entire scientific books have been written on this subject, with more on the way! Basically there are currently two competing theories—the asteroid theory and the gradual decline theory. The asteroid theory states that an asteroid hit the Yucatán Peninsula in the country of Mexico. The resulting fireball and explosion covered Earth with ash that blocked sunlight for years and caused an ecological disaster. The gradual decline theory states that dinosaurs were already near the end of an extinction event when the asteroid finished off the remaining dinosaurs. Both theories have major problems and unanswered questions. The timing of the asteroid impact is most important. Did it hit before, during, or after dinosaurs had reached the point of no return? The studies continue.

CENOZOIC ERA

The final era, which we are in now, is called the Cenozoic (SEN-o-ZO-ick), or "recent life," Era. It began with the continents continuing to split apart (except for India, which crashed into Asia, forming the Himalaya Mountains). Australia separated from Antarctica. North America finally separated from Asia first, then Europe. Mountain-building continued with the formation of the Rocky Mountains, the Andes, and the Alps. The great inland sea across North America retreated, and the Great Plains were formed.

Life as we know it began to take over the Earth. Grasses appeared for the first time, as well as great forests of oak.

Mammals were everywhere, and getting larger. Birds could be found on each of the seven continents. The climate continued to get warmer.

Then, about 3 million years before today, the climate shifted and temperatures dropped. An Ice Age gripped Earth and continent-sized glaciers reshaped the landscape. As the glaciers pushed the surface rocks before them (like a titanic snow shovel), they piled up the debris. One of these piles is today known as Long Island, New York!

As temperatures fluctuated between an ice-covered world at one extreme and warm intervals with retreating glaciers at the other, a new two-legged species of mammal appeared. It was the human race, the most dangerous predators ever to evolve.

Is the Ice Age over? Or are we just in one of the many temporary warm spells? Will the glaciers return, or will human industrial activities (adding pollutants to the atmosphere) send us back to the higher temperatures common in the Cenozoic? Only time will tell.

Plant Life During the Age of Dinosaurs

Most people think of plants as just sort of there, a colorful background. This is far from the truth. Plants are the basis of the food system and have important and dynamic interactions with animals. The evolution of plants is tightly entwined with the evolution of the animals that feed on them.

Being a plant-eating dinosaur wasn't easy. During the Mesozoic Era, or Age of Dinosaurs, plants were harder to digest than modern plants are and provided little nutrition. After a herd of herbivorous, or plant-eating dinosaurs passed through an area, eating up everything in their path, the plant life may have taken a year to grow back. This means that plant-eaters either kept moving around one large region or migrated from region to region. All that extra walking would require more energy, which would require eating more plants, which would require more walking, and so on.

During the Mesozoic Era, there were no grasses, lush jungles, or amber waves of grain. There were, however, club mosses (lycopsids), horsetails (sphenopsids), ferns, seed ferns, cycads, and big trees—the cycadeoids, conifers (cone-bearing trees), and ginkgos. From the Late Triassic (when dinosaurs first appeared) until the Late Cretaceous (when flowering plants started to dominate) these were the only plants a dinosaur could eat. Most of the plants we see today—the angiosperms—did not arrive until the Cretaceous Period.

Plant-eating dinosaurs quickly became the largest animals ever to walk the Earth. This is because they were the first to be able to feed high up in the trees, where the foliage was, without actually having to climb or fly into the trees.

Because the world of the Late Triassic and Jurassic was dominated by cycads and conifers, which were poor in nutrients, plant-eaters developed larger gut areas so they could digest the plants longer to get more nutrients out of them. This left the relatively smaller ornithischians (such as the ornithopods, stegosaurs, and ankylosaurs) to specialize in eating ground cover.

A new food source appeared during the Cretaceous that changed both the landscape and dinosaur evolution. Angiosperms are far more efficient at reproducing and recovering from being eaten than ferns, cycads, and conifers. This meant that angiosperms were better and quicker at growing back in areas cleared by dinosaurs—and they began to push out the older plant groups.

As angiosperms evolved from ground cover into tree-sized plants, so the once smaller plant-eaters evolved into sauropod-sized giants. This new, rapidly growing food source may have been the reason why ornithischians, especially the ornithopods and ceratopsians, began their diversification.

Finding Fossils

How Dinosaurs Are Dug Up

So you want to discover a new dinosaur? How do you start? Well, you can't just go out west, start digging, and expect to find fossils. Digging up fossils is actually a five-part process.

Part 1: Investigation

Before you begin searching for fossils, you need to know where to look. The first step is to find out where sedimentary rocks of the Mesozoic Era (or the Age of Dinosaurs) are now located on the surface of the Earth. This requires a trip to the library. You can research popular books (see the reading list in the back of this book) and old scientific papers by area of interest, geologic formation, and fossil group.

Part 2: Preparation

Once you know where to look, you have to find out who owns the land. Most land in the United States is held by one of six legal types of ownership: federal, state, local government, Native American, corporate, or private. Get permission first! Go to the county seat and look up the Land Records Office. They have maps showing who owns which plots of land.

Next, you will need to assemble your field equipment. For a day trip, the least you will need is water, trail food, a hat, polarized sunglasses, toilet paper, geologic and topographic maps, a ruler, a 35-millimeter camera, a notebook with 100 percent rag paper, number 3 pencils, and a friend. Never go into the badlands alone! And before leaving home, please familiarize yourself with the ethical guidelines of the Society of Vertebrate Paleontology (available at www.vertpaleo.org).

Part 3: Exploration

Assuming you find a dinosaur (which, of course, you are going to give to a school or museum), do not dig it up! First, you must take pictures of the specimen (with the ruler beside it to show size), then map the specific location and the general area.

Accurately plot your location on your maps (ideally using GPS, or global positioning satellite, equipment). Next is the most important part—get a professional vertebrate paleontologist to help unearth your find. Dinosaurs come in literally all sizes, and each different size, and method of preservation, requires a different technique. There is no one-way-fits-all method of excavating fossils—different types of fossil bone even require different glues. Any data lost while digging (for example, ancient pollen samples) is gone forever! This is why a professional is needed. The Society of Vertebrate Paleontology can supply the names of paleontologists in each state and country.

Before digging, set up a grid system around the specimen so you can take more pictures and map exactly where each bone is found. Gradually clear away the surface sediments all around the specimen until there is at least 3 feet of space around each bone. Do not hurry. As each bone is exposed, you'll need to clean it, apply polyvinyl acetates (as shown to you by the paleontologist), and take pictures of each bone.

Using tools provided by the paleontologist, keep digging around the specimen until it is sitting on a pedestal of sediment. Apply a covering of toilet paper or aluminum foil as a separator so the specimen will not stick to the next layer—plaster of Paris reinforced by burlap or a substitute of various linen products.

Then turn the specimen over and repeat the process until it is completely covered. Then take sediment samples from underneath the specimen (where the rock has not been exposed to the air) and seal them in an airtight container. These will be your pollen samples. Label all plaster jackets, boxes, and containers.

The size of the resulting block of rock and plaster will determine how much reinforcing is needed to lift it without breaking it. Wooden planks are generally used for blocks under 500 pounds. (A full description of field techniques can be found in the books listed at the end of this book.) If you are not sure about your technique, then stop and wait for the professional to help.

In the field, near Shell, Wyoming

A dinosaur bone, jacketed with plaster on one side, has just been rolled over so that a jacket can be put on the other side. The bone must be photographed again before it is completely covered.

A dinosaur thighbone has been jacketed with plaster and reinforced with a wooden plank. Other bones are being jacketed.

This is the pubis of an immature sauropod dinosaur inside a field jacket of plaster of Paris and burlap.

Bones of a sauropod dinosaur are exposed and conserved. One person is applying a layer of plaster of Paris and burlap to protect the bones for shipment back to the museum.

Here's where things start getting expensive. You'll need to get your fossils back to the lab. In general, a truck will do the job, but depending on your location, you may need a helicopter!

Get lots of money to rent a proper-sized vehicle. Make sure your find is securely packed to withstand the bumps and jolts of the ride home. Keep records of everything packed up and everything shipped. Clean the excavation site and backfill all holes. As spelunkers, or cave explorers, say, "Take only pictures, leave only footprints."

Write up everything you did, who did what, and what pictures were taken, then put all the information in your field book. Give credit where credit is due.

*

This is a very simplified explanation. That is because it would take a book to describe all the finer details of excavation and how they vary depending upon what is found.

Fossil footprints require a different procedure, and so do microvertebrates like lizards and mammals. It is best to go on an expedition run by a school or museum before going off on your own. Books listed at the back of this book will tell you where you can apply to go on a dig.

How Dinosaurs
Are Prepared

Once a specimen is back in the lab, the preparator opens the plaster of Paris field jacket, then gently removes the surrounding rock from the fossil using dental drills and scrapers. Many of these instruments are the same ones used by dentists and artists. (Shown is preparator Steve Jabo of the National Museum of Natural History in Washington, D.C.)

There are many different kinds of glues and preservatives. Which one to use depends on how the bone is preserved and on the chemicals that may be present within.

To conserve large fossil bones in museum collections, new plaster jackets are lined with foam to keep the bone from rubbing against the hard plaster. Foam is also added into open spaces, making the fit between the bones and the jacket nice and snug. Metal rods are used to add strength to the jacket. The preparator then glues and fills any cracks in the bones.

To protect the largest specimens that will not fit into museum storage drawers, metal-reinforced plaster jackets lined with foam are custom-made into protective "clamshells." These shells allow specimens to be flipped over for study while keeping them supported from below. A catalog number is written on each jacket to identify the bones within.

To mount a skeleton, each bone must be individually fitted onto a metal frame. Extra metal bars and plates are sometimes added for increased strength. Preparators must know about metal welding and casting techniques, in addition to their knowledge of chemicals, preservatives, preparation methods, and molding.

The main support for a mount of an entire dinosaur is a metal "backbone," to which the other bones will be attached.

All fossil bones need periodic cleaning and regluing. Changes in temperature or humidity, or vibrations from traffic, can cause new cracks to appear. The conservation of fossils is an ongoing process that is necessary to preserve our natural heritage for future generations.

How Dinosaurs Are Classified

What if you found a dinosaur fossil? How would you figure out what type of dinosaur it was? First you would have to compare your fossil's features to the features of other dinosaurs it most closely resembled. In other words, you would have to "classify" your dinosaur.

Scientists have developed a complex system for classifying all living things. Each species is part of a larger group. For example, lions and tigers are part of the cat family (or Felidae), and the cat family and the dog family (or Canidae) are both part of the shearing-toothed mammal group (or Carnivora). Likewise, the dinosaurs *Anatotitan* and *Parasaurolophus* are both part of the duckbilled dinosaur family (or Hadrosauridae), and the hadrosaurs and horned dinosaurs are both part of the bird-hipped dinosaurs (or Ornithischia).

Other dinosaurs in this book can be classified under other families based on their similarities and shared ancestry. And all of these families can be classified under the largest group of all—Dinosauria.

Keep in mind that not all ancient creatures were dinosaurs. For example, marine reptiles were not dinosaurs (see plesiosaurs and ichthyosaurs on pages 135 and 136). Neither were pterosaurs (see pages 145–150). And neither were various groups of extinct furry mammals— such as woolly mammoths and saber-toothed cats—and their relatives.

To a scientist, a dinosaur is any descendant of the most recent common ancestor of *Iguanodon* and *Megalosaurus*. The following pages will show you one possible way to classify dinosaurs. It is accepted by many paleontologists today. Note, however, that new discoveries sometimes suggest new relationships between groups of dinosaurs. In years to come, therefore, depending on new discoveries, the classifications on the next pages may change quite a bit!

DINOSAURIA

(all dinosaurs)

Members of this group have limbs aimed directly beneath the body, an open space in the hip socket, and a special grasping hand (at least in the earliest forms). Dinosauria is divided into two groups: Saurischia and Ornithischia. Each group of dinosaurs evolved in its own way, and over time the groups became very different from each other.

ORNITHISCHIA

(bird-hipped dinosaurs)

These dinosaurs have a backward-pointing pubis bone in their hips, which made room for the extra guts needed to digest plants, and an extra bone in the front of their lower jaw, which formed the bottom part of their beak. As far as paleontologists know, ornithischians were all herbivores, or plant-eaters. Ornithischia includes three major groups: Thyreophora, Marginocephalia, and Ornithopoda.

•graph continues on next page•

SAURISCHIA

(lizard-hipped dinosaurs)

These dinosaurs have longer necks than ornithischians and hands that were much better for grasping. In most saurischians, the pubic bone in the pelvis points forward. Saurischia is divided into the Sauropodomorpha, which were plant-eaters, and the Theropoda, which were mostly meat-eaters.

•graph continues on next page•

ORNITHISCHIA
(bird-hipped dinosaurs)

These dinosaurs have a backward-pointing pubis bone in their hips, which made roor for the extra guts needed to digest plants, and an extra bone in the front of their lowe jaw, which formed the bottom part of their beak. As far as paleontologists knov ornithischians were all herbivores, or plant-eaters. Ornithischia includes three majo groups: Thyreophora, Marginocephalia, and Ornithopoda.

THYREOPHORA
(armored dinosaurs)

Thyreophorans have bony armor in their skin to protect them from attackers. Most can be put into one of two groups:

MARGINOCEPHALIA
(ridge-headed dinosaurs)

Marginocephalians are a group c ornithischians with a shelf of bone o the back of the skull. They include tw major groups:

Ceratopsia
(frilled, horned dinosaurs)

Early members of the frilled dinosaur: (such as *Archaeoceratops*) lacked horns while the later, heavily built quadrupeda ceratopsians (such as *Centrosaurus*) hac horns.

Ankylosauria
(tank dinosaurs)

Ankylosaurs are tank-like dinosaurs. Examples include club-tailed forms, like *Ankylosaurus*, and clubless ones, like *Edmontonia*, *Gargoyleosaurus*, and *Gastonia*.

Stegosauria
(plated dinosaurs)

Stegosaurs are plated dinosaurs with rows of armored plates and spikes down their backs. Examples include *Kentrosaurus*, *Stegosaurus*, and *Wuerhosaurus*.

A U R I A

SAURISCHIA
·explained on next page·

ORNITHOPODA
(beaked dinosaurs)

Ornithopods were ornithischians with special teeth, some with multiple rows of teeth, to help them chew. Many primitive ornithopods (such as *Dryosaurus, Gasparinisaura,* and *Thescelosaurus*) were relatively small and walked only on their hind legs, while more advanced ones (such as *Altirhinus, Iguanodon,* and *Muttaburrasaurus*) were much larger and spent a lot of time walking on all fours.

Pachycephalosauria
(thick-headed dinosaurs)

Pachycephalosaurs are thick-headed reptiles with solid domes of bone. They include *Prenocephale, Homalocephale,* and *Pachycephalosaurus*.

Hadrosauridae
(duckbilled dinosaurs)

Hadrosaurs are the largest and most specialized of all the ornithopods. This group includes *Anatotitan, Corythosaurus, Hadrosaurus, Parasaurolophus,* and *Prosaurolophus*.

D I N O S

ORNITHISCHIA
·explained on previous page·

THEROPODA
(meat-eating dinosaurs)

These dinosaurs are a very diverse group. All theropods walked on their hind legs, ar
all but the most primitive have a wishbone.

Tetanurae
(stiff-tailed theropods)

Tetanurines generally have bigger hands than ceratosaurs. They include the giant carnosaurs (such as *Allosaurus* and *Giganotosaurus*), the crocodile-snouted spinosaurids (such as *Spinosaurus* and *Suchomimus*), and more primitive forms (such as *Metriacanthosaurus*).

Ceratosauria
(primitive theropods)

Ceratosaurs are all small to large two footed meat-eaters with fused ank bones. They include giants such as th abelisaurs (including *Abelisaurus* ar *Carnotaurus*) and smaller, more slende hunters such as *Procompsognathus*.

Coelurosauria
(coelurosaurs)

Coelurosaurs are the most advanced and diverse group of tetanurines. They have variou specialized features of the skeleton, and (apparently) a very unusual feature of the ski Recent discoveries show that most (if not all) coelurosaurs had feathers during at leas part of their life! There are many groups of coelurosaurs:

Primitive forms,
such as little *Compsogna-thus, Nqwebasaurus,* and *Sinosauropteryx.*

Tyrannosauridae
(tyrant dinosaurs)

These are giant two-fingered hunters, such as *Gorgosaurus* and *Tyrannosaurus.*

Ornithomimosauria
(ostrich dinosaurs)

These are small-headed, lon necked runners, such a *Gallimimus* and *Pelecanimimu*

AURIA

SAURISCHIA
(lizard-hipped dinosaurs)

nese dinosaurs have longer necks than ornithischians and hands that were much better
r grasping. In most saurischians, the pubic bone in the pelvis points forward. Saurischia
divided into the Sauropodomorpha, which were plant-eaters, and the Theropoda,
hich were mostly meat-eaters.

SAUROPODOMORPHA
(long-necked dinosaurs)

nese dinosaurs had very long necks and small heads. This allowed them to feed higher
the bushes and trees than other dinosaurs.

Prosauropoda
(before the Sauropoda)

osauropods are primitive, or early,
uropodomorphs. They were plant-
ters that could walk on their hind
gs or on all fours. Prosauropods
clude *Plateosaurus.*

Sauropoda
(giant long-necked dinosaurs)

Sauropods came later than the
prosauropods and were so large they
could walk only on all fours. Sauropods
include *Apatosaurus, Argentinosaurus,* and
Brachiosaurus.

Maniraptora (maniraptors)

ncludes: long-necked, plant-eating Therizinosauroidae ("sloth dinosaurs"), such as
Beipiaosaurus; short-skulled, beaked Oviraptorosauria ("egg thieves"), such as *Caudipteryx;*
arge-brained, big-eyed Troodontidae ("troodonts"), including *Troodon;* Dromaeosauridae
"raptors"), such as *Velociraptor;* strange, short-armed Alvarezsauridae ("alvarezsaurs"),
ncluding *Shuvuuia;* and Avialae (birds), such as *Archaeopteryx.*

How Dinosaurs Are Named

Have you ever wondered how dinosaurs are named? Let's say you dig up a new dinosaur. What would you do then? You can't just call your local newspaper and announce the new name. It would not be considered valid by scientists around the world.

Instead, to properly name your discovery, you must follow a scientific procedure guided by international laws. Specifically, your new dinosaur must meet the requirements set up by the International Committee of Zoological Nomenclature (ICZN).

(1) First, you must write a scientific paper that explains the unique features of the dinosaur you found. The paper will explain to the world exactly why your dinosaur is new to science.

(2) You must have your paper published in a scientific journal or book.

(3) The original specimen that you dug up (known as the type specimen) must be conserved by a museum that is expected to exist beyond the lifetime of its current employees, such as the museums that meet the standards of the American Association of Museums.

(4) The type specimen must also be made available for study by other scientists.

But before you write your paper, how do you decide on the name itself?

Your new dinosaur's name should be based on Latin or ancient Greek. In general, the genus name refers to a feature of the dinosaur (such as *Tyrannosaurus,* or "tyrant lizard"). The species name can refer back to the genus (as does *Tyrannosaurus rex—rex* meaning "king," so the name means "king of the tyrant lizards"), or it can refer to a place or a person. (For example, *Lambeosaurus lambei* was named after Lawrence Lambe, a famous Canadian paleontologist.)

A good scientific paper is written so that it can be read by paleontologists who have not yet been born. You might think of it as a set of directions on how to repeat what you did, so that the steps you took can be repeated and tested by others in the future.

The whole process of writing a scientific paper can take from a few months to a few years. No profit is ever made. (In fact, the author has to pay for the paper to be published. These are called "page charges" and can be as high as two hundred dollars a page!) Indeed, it can cost thousands of dollars in labor, material, and time. So why do we do it? Because paleontologists are also educators. It is our job to find new discoveries about the deep past—and then tell the world!

DRAWING DINOSAURS

Any time you see an extinct dinosaur drawn with flesh on the bone and skin on the flesh, you are seeing a bit of "science fiction." Like the best science fiction, these drawings are based on science fact, but a lot of imagination and guesswork goes into them. Bob Walters' illustrations in this book represent various ideas about what dinosaurs (and other ancient beasts) looked like. In order to draw dinosaurs, Bob—and artists like him— go through the following steps:

• They reconstruct the skeletons of the dinosaur. Missing bones are restored based on comparisons with closely related dinosaurs.

• They fill in the muscles of the skeleton. These are based on muscle scars found on bones, and/or on comparisons with living animals.

• They place skin over the muscles.

• They "clothe" the skin in scales and/or feathers. All dinosaurs had scales on parts of their bodies, but the exact shape and pattern of the scales is known for only a few species. Also, in the late 1990s it was discovered that some (if not all) of the small, swift meat-eating dinosaurs had feathers, or hair-like "protofeathers." Scientists currently have

specific knowledge of some of the
feathers found on small meat-eaters from
only one geological formation in China.

For now, the shape and size of these
features in all other creatures is
guesswork.

• They add color to the scales
and/or feathers. Colors and
patterns used by artists are pure
speculation, because nature is full of all different
colored animals. (For example, the skeletons of
lions, tigers, and leopards are nearly identical,
but they have totally different colors and color
patterns. Without seeing the
living great cats, we would
never know of a lion's mane, a
tiger's stripes, or a leopard's
spots.)

But remember: Although we
know what the
skeletons of Tyrannosaurus and
Velociraptor looked like, we
will never know for sure how
their outsides appeared. Unless,
of course, Jurassic Park turns out
to be more than a story. . . .

ABELISAURUS
a-BEL-i-SAWR-us
(year named: 1985)

FUN FACTS: Possible relatives of *Abelisaurus* are known from Spain and France.

LOCATION: Rio Negro Province, Argentina

FOOD: Other dinosaurs (titanosaurs, hadrosaurs, and small ornithopods)

SIZE: Perhaps about 26 feet (7.9 m) long, perhaps 6.6 feet (2 m) high at the hips

WEIGHT: About 1.4 tons

FRIENDS: None

ENEMIES: *Carnotaurus*

TRIVIA: More species of fossil dinosaurs have been found in Argentina than any other country in the Southern Hemisphere.

Abelisaurus ("[Roberto] Abel's lizard") was one of the top predators in South America at the end of the Age of Dinosaurs. While *Tyrannosaurus* and its kin dominated the northern continents during the Late Cretaceous, the abelisaurs ruled South America, India, and Madagascar.

Like the tyrannosaurs, abelisaurs had big skulls with knobby snouts. Unlike the tyrannosaurs, however, abelisaurs had teeth that were fairly small. The rounded snout of *Abelisaurus* and its relatives probably helped it to hold on to what it was biting. Its fused skull roof made its head hard enough to be used as a weapon in fights between rival abelisaurs. By pushing each other with their heads, one *Abelisaurus* could try to defeat the other without having to face attack by claws or jaws.

Abelisaurus is known at present only from a single giant skull, over 33 inches (85 cm) long.

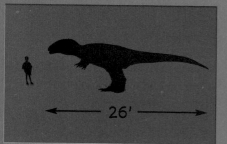

← 26' →

Comparison is with a 4-foot child

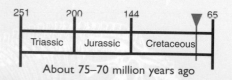

251	200	144	▼ 65
Triassic	Jurassic	Cretaceous	

About 75–70 million years ago

ALLOSAURUS
AL-o-SAWR-us
(year named: 1877)

Allosaurus ("other lizard") was the most common predator of the Late Jurassic and probably one of the most dangerous. Like most meat-eating dinosaurs, its jaws were filled with serrated teeth shaped like blades. Computer studies suggest that *Allosaurus* attacked by using its upper jaw like a battle ax to hack at its victim, then it used its lower jaw to bite out a slice of meat.

It might have been easy for an *Allosaurus* to kill a fairly defenseless dinosaur like *Camptosaurus*, but *Stegosaurus* could certainly put up a fight, and the sauropods (giant long-necks) were so huge that they could easily crush even an adult *Allosaurus*.

We know that *Allosaurus* led a dangerous life. The *Allosaurus* on display at the Smithsonian Institution has a smashed shoulder blade, many broken ribs, and a lower jaw so damaged that paleontologists didn't realize it was an *Allosaurus* jaw for over 100 years! But these were tough dinosaurs: Their bones show that they lived long enough for their wounds to heal.

FUN FACTS: The first fossil of *Allosaurus* ever found—the broken half of a backbone—was called a petrified horse hoof by its discoverers!

LOCATION: Montana, Wyoming, Colorado, New Mexico, Oklahoma, Utah, South Dakota, Portugal

FOOD: Other dinosaurs

SIZE: 40 feet (12 m) long, about 10 feet (3 m) high at the hips

WEIGHT: About 4.5 tons

FRIENDS: None

ENEMIES: *Stegosaurus, Torvosaurus, Saurophaganax, Ceratosaurus*

TRIVIA: *Allosaurus* is the official state dinosaur of Utah.

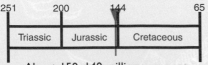

251	200	144	65
Triassic	Jurassic	Cretaceous	

About 150–140 million years ago

← 40' →

Comparison is with a 4-foot child

ALTIRHINUS
al-tee-RIEN-us
(year named: 1998)

FUN FACTS: With its expanded nose, *Altirhinus* may have been the first dinosaur to "hoot" like a woodwind instrument.
LOCATION: Mongolia
FOOD: Possibly early flowering plants, cycads, and ginkgos
SIZE: 24 feet (8 m) long, 6.6 feet (2 m) high at the hips
WEIGHT: 4 tons
FRIENDS: *Psittacosaurus*
ENEMIES: *Harpymimus*
TRIVIA: The original *Altirhinus* skull (minus the body) went on a world tour in the late 1990s.

Altirhinus ("high nose") had an enlarged-beak and mouth to help it eat tough plants. This expanded nose may also have improved *Altirhinus*'s sense of smell and helped it recognize the same species during mating season. (Among the *Altirhinus,* a big nose was considered very attractive!)

Altirhinus is referred to as being "more than an *Iguanodon,* but less than a hadrosaur" because the body is like *Iguanodon*'s, but the skull is closer to that of the duckbills. In fact, *Altirhinus* is a good example of how difficult it sometimes is to classify finds. For years, this dinosaur was known as *Iguanodon orientalis*. Named by a Russian scientist in 1952, *Iguanodon orientalis*—which was found in Mongolia—was thought to be in the same genus as the original *Iguanodon,* which was found in Britain. Although the bodies of the two *are* similar, the skulls are very different. It was not until 1998 that David Norman, an authority on the family Iguanodontidae, revised the taxonomy of *Iguanodon* and finally gave *I. orientalis* its new name—*Altirhinus kurzanovi.*

← 24' →

Comparison is with a 4-foot child

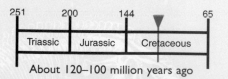

251	200	144	65
Triassic	Jurassic	Cretaceous	

About 120–100 million years ago

36

AMARGASAURUS
a-MAHR-gah-SAWR-us
(year named: 1991)

Amargasaurus ("lizard from La Amarga [geologic formation]") is one of the most unusual sauropods known to science. Its most distinguishing feature is the tall double row of spines, like two sails, coming out of the back of its neck. These sails served many functions—at a price. They made the dinosaur look much bigger than it was, possibly keeping predators away. The sails could also be used—under certain conditions—like a solar panel, gathering heat when facing into the sun and losing heat when in the shade. Unfortunately, the sails were also very restrictive and would severely limit the range of motion in Amargasaurus's head and neck. They were also very fragile and would get seriously damaged if bitten.

FUN FACTS: Some Amargasaurus neck spines are 19.6 inches (50 cm) long.

LOCATION: Patagonia, Argentina

FOOD: Conifers, cycads, ginkgos

SIZE: 30 feet (9 m) long, 8 feet (2.5 m) high at the hip

WEIGHT: 15 tons

TRIVIA: The only mounted skeleton in the world is in Buenos Aires, Argentina.

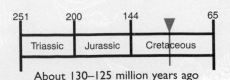

251	200	144		65
Triassic	Jurassic	Cretaceous		

About 130–125 million years ago

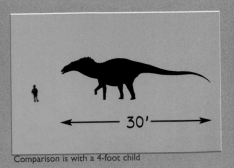

30'

Comparison is with a 4-foot child

ANATOTITAN

a-NAT-o-TIE-tan

(year named: 1990)

FUN FACTS: *Anatotitan* was first found in 1904, and renamed in 1990. There are fewer than 10 known *Anatotitan* skeletons—far less than the hundreds of skeletons known for its closest relative, *Edmontosaurus*.

LOCATION: South Dakota

FOOD: Plants

SIZE: 33 feet (10 m) long, 8 feet (2.5 m) high at the hips

WEIGHT: 5 tons

FRIENDS: *Edmontosaurus*, *Thescelosaurus*

ENEMIES: *Tyrannosaurus*, *Dromaeosaurus*

TRIVIA: This is the "typical duckbill" made famous by the paintings of the "Father of Paleoart," Charles R. Knight.

Anatotitan ("duck titan") was the largest non-crested duckbill in North America. Its name refers to its duck-like beak. *Anatotitan* is part of the Hadrosauridae, or duckbill family of dinosaurs, who are known for their amazing teeth—or as paleontologists call it, their "dental battery." On each side of *Anatotitan*'s jaw are three rows of sixty or more perfectly interlocking teeth—that's 720 per mouth, compared to thirty-two in an adult human! Not only did *Anatotitan* have a *lot* of teeth, but when one fell out, another from inside its jaw would take its place! Teeth like these are called "evergrowing."

Anatotitan ate plants and had to be on constant alert for predators such as *Tyrannosaurus* and *Dromaeosaurus*. *Anatotitan* could not outrun any of the meat-eaters and had to rely on out-maneuvering them—like a crafty football player—or traveling in large herds, where there was safety in numbers.

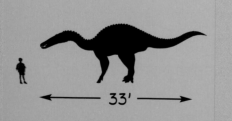

← 33' →

Comparison is with a 4-foot child

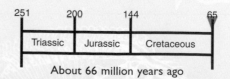

251	200	144	65
Triassic	Jurassic	Cretaceous	

About 66 million years ago

38

ANKYLOSAURUS
ANG-ki-lo-SAWR-us
(year named: 1908)

Ankylosaurus ("fused lizard") is the name-bearer for the group of dinosaurs known as the Ankylosauria, or "tank dinosaurs." They're called "tanks" because the upper parts of their bodies are covered with various types of armor that are fused together.

The armor of ankylosaurs can be either solid or hollow. It is found on top of their bodies and tails, and also all around the skull—imagine putting on a football helmet and having your skin grow over it! This extreme level of defense was necessary because no ankylosaur could outrun a theropod, or meat-eating dinosaur. In 1998, another new species of ankylosaur was named. It was called *Animantarx* ("living fortress").

In *Ankylosaurus,* the last half of the tail has been modified into a giant war club, with the last tail bones fused together. When this club was swung from side to side, it was at the same level as the knees of theropods like *Tyrannosaurus.* How's that for strategically placed weaponry!

FUN FACTS: *Ankylosaurus* had eight sinus cavities, as compared to only four in nodosaurs (and also in humans).
LOCATION: Montana; Wyoming; Alberta, Canada
FOOD: Flowering plants like magnolias, possibly small insects
SIZE: 25 feet (7.5 m) long, 4 feet (1.2 m) high at the hips
WEIGHT: 3 tons
TRIVIA: *Ankylosaurus* was the last of the Thyreophora ("shield-bearers," a group that includes the ankylosaurs and stegosaurs). The earliest was *Scelidosaurus.*

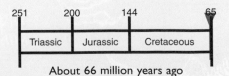

251	200	144	65
Triassic	Jurassic	Cretaceous	

About 66 million years ago

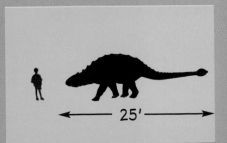

25'

Comparison is with a 4-foot child

39

Apatosaurus
a-PAT-o-SAWR-us

(year named: 1877)

FUN FACTS: One species of *Apatosaurus* was named after a millionaire's wife in the hope it would bring more funding!

LOCATION: From Oklahoma to Canada along the Rocky Mountains

FOOD: Cycads, ginkgos, ferns, conifers

SIZE: About 70 feet (21 m) long, 10 feet (3 m) high at the hips

WEIGHT: 25 tons

Apatosaurus ("deceptive lizard") looks very much like *Diplodocus,* its closest relative. On the inside, however, it is very different. *Apatosaurus* is very massive, with thick bones and a stocky body. *Diplodocus* is slender, with thinner bones. *Apatosaurus* was one of the very first dinosaurs to have a picture of its completely restored skeleton published in newspapers. This happened in the 1880s, and the dinosaur's immense size made world headlines.

One feature that *Apatosaurus* has in common with other closely related sauropods, or giant plant-eaters, is that the openings for its nostrils are on top of its head, behind its eyes. (Normally nostrils are located at the end of the snout, as in the Ornithischia, the other major group of plant-eating dinosaurs.) This setup enabled *Apatosaurus* to breathe through an air passage to the rear of its throat—like a human—making it possible to chew a mouthful of plants and breathe at the same time. If you want to see why this is important, pinch your own nose closed and try chewing without breathing through your mouth. Be careful not to choke!

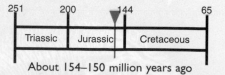

251	200	144	65
Triassic	Jurassic	Cretaceous	

About 154–150 million years ago

The study of *Apatosaurus* has had a major influence on the study of all dinosaurs. In the 1970s, a study of its skeleton was used to show how sauropods lived on land, and not in the water as had been assumed for many decades. In 1979, it was learned that the wrong head had been mounted on every *Apatosaurus* skeleton in museums since the 1880s (the older mounts had heads based on *Camarasaurus*). In the 1990s, a study of *Apatosaurus* bones showed that its head and neck were not held vertically as had been portrayed in many illustrations. The science of how a body can or cannot function is called functional morphology, and *Apatosaurus* is one of the best dinosaurs for use in this study because of its large size.

FRIENDS: *Diplodocus, Camarasaurus*

ENEMIES: *Allosaurus, Ceratosaurus, Torvosaurus*

TRIVIA: *Apatosaurus* was once considered to be a different animal from the sauropod called *Brontosaurus*. Now we know they are the same dinosaur.

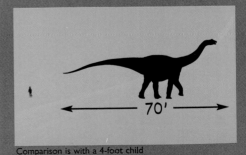

70'

Comparison is with a 4-foot child

ARCHAEOCERATOS
AHR-kee-o-SAIR-a-tops

(year named: 1997)

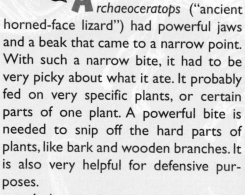

FUN FACTS: This small dinosaur might have been able to outrun a teacher. (How fast can *your* teacher run?)

LOCATION: Gansu Province, China

FOOD: Plants

SIZE: About 2.5 feet (72 cm) long, 1.25 feet (35 cm) high at the hips

WEIGHT: 50 pounds

FRIENDS: Other ceratopsians and small ankylosaurs

ENEMIES: Juveniles of any theropods, or meat-eating dinosaurs

TRIVIA: Even though *Archeoceratops*'s skull was the same size as a dog's, it had much more powerful jaws.

Archaeoceratops ("ancient horned-face lizard") had powerful jaws and a beak that came to a narrow point. With such a narrow bite, it had to be very picky about what it ate. It probably fed on very specific plants, or certain parts of one plant. A powerful bite is needed to snip off the hard parts of plants, like bark and wooden branches. It is also very helpful for defensive purposes.

Archaeoceratops is one of the earliest horned dinosaurs from Asia, if not *the* earliest. Only two skeletons have been "published" so far, so questions (and there are many!) about its age must wait for further study by both paleontologists and geologists.

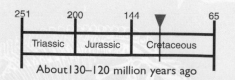

←2.5'→

Comparison is with a 4-foot child

251	200	144		65
Triassic	Jurassic	Cretaceous		

About 130–120 million years ago

ARCHAEOPTERYX
AHR-kee-OP-ter-iks
(year named: 1861)

FUN FACTS: The shape of the feathers on *Archaeopteryx*'s wings show that it was capable of flying, but probably not well.

LOCATION: Germany, possibly Portugal

FOOD: Small mammals and reptiles

SIZE: Almost 20 inches (50 cm) long, 7.5 inches (19 cm) high at the hips, wingspan about 2 feet (61 cm)

WEIGHT: Possibly 14 ounces (400 g)

TRIVIA: All known skeletons of this early bird were found in rocks formed from soft limy mud. It was this very fine mud that preserved the impressions of their feathers. If *Archaeopteryx* had been preserved in another environment, we might never have known it had feathers!

Archaeopteryx ("ancient wing") is the oldest and most primitive known bird. It is also one of the most important fossils ever found.

Archaeopteryx shows a mixture of features found in birds (like a wishbone, feathers, and backward-facing pubis bone in the hips), as well as features found in primitive reptiles but lost in modern birds (like teeth, clawed fingers, and a long, bony tail). As more dinosaur skeletons were found (especially those of smaller meat-eaters), paleontologists began to notice that they shared many of the same features with the much smaller *Archaeopteryx*. These features included wishbones, feathers, and a backward-facing pubis bone. Scientists figured out that *Archaeopteryx* and other birds are the descendants of small meat-eating dinosaurs, and in fact (using the modern system of classification), birds are a type of dinosaur themselves!

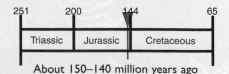

251	200	144	65
Triassic	Jurassic	Cretaceous	

About 150–140 million years ago

19"

Comparison is with a 4-foot child

BARYONYX
BAR-ee-ON-iks
(year named: 1986)

Baryonyx ("heavy claw") was discovered by an amateur fossil hunter, William J. Walker, who came across its enormous thumb claw in a clay pit in Surrey, England. Further digging by paleontologists revealed one of the largest meat-eating dinosaurs ever found in Great Britain.

Baryonyx is a spinosaur, a member of the same group as the northern African dinosaurs Spinosaurus and Suchomimus. Baryonyx was smaller than these relatives but was still a big predator. It had a long, narrow snout filled with teeth that were cone-shaped—a real difference from the blade-shaped teeth of typical meat-eating dinosaurs.

Because of the shape of its snout and teeth (both of which are similar to those of modern crocodiles and alligators), some paleontologists think that Baryonyx ate lots of fish. Others, however, think that it ate other dinosaurs. In fact, both ideas are supported by the original Baryonyx specimen from Surrey. In the guts of this dinosaur, paleontologists found the partially digested scales of large fish as well as the partially digested bones of a young Iguanodon. This strongly supports the idea that Baryonyx ate both fish *and* dinosaurs!

FUN FACTS: Baryonyx was given the nickname "Claws" because of its giant thumb claw.
LOCATION: Surrey, England
FOOD: Other dinosaurs (including Iguanodon) and fish
SIZE: 33 feet (10 m) long, 8 feet (2.5 m) high at the hips
WEIGHT: 1.7 tons
FRIENDS: None
ENEMIES: Neovenator
TRIVIA: Baryonyx is the only definite spinosaur known from a northern continent.

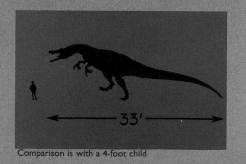

—— 33' ——

Comparison is with a 4-foot child

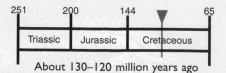

251	200	144	▼	65
Triassic	Jurassic	Cretaceous		

About 130–120 million years ago

44

BEIPIAOSAURUS
bay-pyow-SAWR-us

(year named: 1999)

Beipiaosaurus ("Beipiao lizard") is one of the therizinosaurs, a very strange group of theropods. Therizinosaurs (also known as "sloth dinosaurs") have very short, heavy feet, wide bellies, long necks, big claws, and small heads at the end of long necks. Their teeth are leaf-shaped, like those of plant-eating dinosaurs, which makes them plant-eating members of the family of meat-eating dinosaurs!

Beipiaosaurus is known from one partial skeleton from the Yixian Formation in northeastern China. The volcanic ash that formed the mud of this formation was so fine-grained that it preserved very small details of the animals buried in it.

Fossils show that Beipiaosaurus's body was covered with long, slender filaments. These filaments were a sort of protofeather, a body cover that eventually evolved into true feathers in birds and some other dinosaurs (such as Caudipteryx). The protofeathers of Beipiaosaurus might have been used for insulation or for display, or for both.

FUN FACTS:
Beipiaosaurus is the smallest known therizinosaur. Its giant relative *Therizinosaurus* was almost as big as *T. rex* and had claws almost 3 feet (90 cm) long!

LOCATION: Liaoning Province, China

FOOD: Conifers, cycads, ginkgos, the earliest flowering plants

SIZE: 7.3 feet (2.2 m) long, just under 3 feet (0.88 m) high at the hips

WEIGHT: Perhaps 187 lbs (85 kg)

TRIVIA: *Beipiaosaurus* is the first therizinosaur known to have protofeathers.

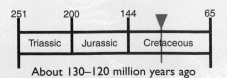

251	200	144	65
Triassic	Jurassic	Cretaceous	

About 130–120 million years ago

← 7.3' →

Comparison is with a 4-foot child

BRACHIOSAURUS
BRAK-ee-o-SAWR-us
(year named: 1903)

Brachiosaurus ("arm lizard") one of the most spectacular dinosa ever seen. It gets its name from great height of its humerus, or upp arm bone—which is longer than m humans are tall! Originally discovered 1900 in Colorado, *Brachiosaurus* v named in 1903 by Elmer Riggs of t Field Museum in Chicago.

For almost a century, *Brachiosau* was considered the tallest of all din saurs. It was over 50 feet (15 m) tall, a no other animal came close. Imagi going to the fifth floor of a building a looking down at the sidewalk. No imagine your feet are at street lev and this is how tall you are! Get t idea? Today, however, there is a new co tender for the title of tallest dinosaur. It is *Sauroposeidon,* named in 2000. Scien-

FUN FACTS: *Brachiosaurus* lived in both the United States and Africa during the Jurassic. Because *Brachiosaurus* would have been a terrible swimmer, this shows scientists that Africa and North America were connected during the Jurassic.

LOCATION: Colorado, Tanzania, possibly Portugal

FOOD: Conifers, cycads, ginkgos

SIZE: 80 feet (24 m) long, 23 feet (7 m) high at the hips

WEIGHT: 30 tons

FRIENDS: *Camarasaurus, Dicraeosaurus*

ENEMIES: *Allosaurus, Ceratosaurus, Elaphrosaurus*

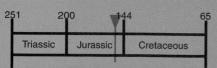

251	200	144	65
Triassic	Jurassic	Cretaceous	

About 150–140 million years ago

ists believe it would stand 60 eet (18 m) tall!

New studies by computer pecialists suggest that *Brahiosaurus* may not have caried its neck angled up as high s was once thought. It may ave carried the neck more at . 45- to 60-degree angle. Although this changes its eight, it does not change ts length—or our won-ler at this gigantic, raceful dinosaur.

TRIVIA: *Brachiosaurus* was one of the few dinosaurs that was literally too big to attack!

TAKE TWO!
The scene in Jurassic Park where you first see *Brachiosaurus* is considered to be the best film restoration of this dinosaur in the 20th century.

←— 80' —→

Comparison is with a 4-foot child

CAMARASAURUS
KAM-ah-ra-SAWR-us
(year named: 1877)

Camarasaurus ("chambered lizard") is one of the most bulky of the sauropods, the big long-necked plant-eaters. It has teeth that are shaped like spoons, only much thicker. The head is large and boxlike, with powerful jaws and a wide bite. *Camarasaurus* fed on very tough, fibrous plants and, like all sauropods, did not chew food but swallowed it whole. This is why sauropods swallowed gastroliths, or stomach stones. The stones helped to grind up the plants inside their stomachs.

The name *Camarasaurus* comes from the chambers that can be seen in its vertebrae. These hollow chambers serve to lighten the skeleton and give it strength. Some scientists believe that these chambers also housed an air-sac system similar to that in birds. Air sacs are part of the respiratory system and are connected to the lungs. This would have greatly helped the air flow through the lungs. Gigantic animals like sauropods would have benefited from a more efficient system of breathing, because carrying around over twenty-five tons of weight would require a lot of oxygen.

FUN FACTS: *Camarasaurus* is one of the very few dinosaurs for which juvenile skeletons have been found along with adults.
LOCATION: Colorado, Wyoming, Utah, New Mexico, Montana, Portugal (?)
FOOD: conifers, cycads, ginkgos
SIZE: 50 feet (15 m) long, 7 feet (2.1 m) high at the hips
WEIGHT: 25 tons
TRIVIA: This dinosaur was part of the famous "Bone Wars" of the 1870s between Edward Drinker Cope and Othniel C. Marsh, two scientists who competed to name the most dinosaurs.

← 50' →

Comparison is with a 4-foot child

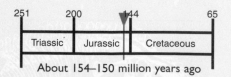

251	200	144	65
Triassic	Jurassic	Cretaceous	

About 154–150 million years ago

CAMPTOSAURUS
KAMP-to-SAWR-us
(year named: 1879)

Camptosaurus ("bent lizard") is one of the ornithopods, or beaked dinosaurs. It gets its name from the fact that its thighbone is very slightly bent outward. This is common in many small bipedal dinosaurs. It is an adaptation to get the thighbone out and away from the rib cage while walking, increasing the freedom of movement. A quick escape was *Camptosaurus's* best defense against predators.

Camptosaurus is important in the study of the ornithopods because it represents the first step in a series of adaptations that eventually resulted in the hadrosaurs (duckbilled dinosaurs). In it we can see the first adaptations for carrying a large, heavy body (a thicker, wider pelvis) and the first indications of a staggered row of teeth (instead of a single row).

As far as we can tell, *Camptosaurus* was rare. Few specimens have been found, and no complete specimens. This may be because it lived in the Morrison Formation, along the Rocky Mountains. This formation is famous for its predators. A relatively small dinosaur like *Camptosaurus* would have made a good meal, and its remains would have been easily scavenged.

FUN FACTS: The camptosaurs were the closest relatives of the iguanodons.
LOCATION: Wyoming, Utah, Colorado, Oklahoma, possibly Europe
FOOD: Conifers, cycads, ginkgos, horsetails
SIZE: 15 feet (4.5 m) long, 5 feet (1.5 m) high at the hips
WEIGHT: .5 ton
TRIVIA: The original specimens used to name two species of *Camptosaurus* are on display at the Smithsonian Institution in Washington, D.C.

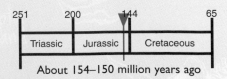

251	200		144	65
	Triassic	Jurassic	Cretaceous	

About 154–150 million years ago

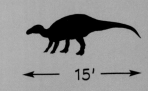

15'

Comparison is with a 4-foot child

CARCHARODONTOSAURUS

kahr-KAR-o-DON-to-SAWR-us

(year named: 1931)

FUN FACTS: *Carcharodontosaurus* had a very narrow skull. Because its eyes faced sideways, it wouldn't have been able to focus well on things right in front of it, but it could have seen almost all its surroundings at once.

LOCATION: Morocco, Niger, Egypt

FOOD: Other dinosaurs (titanosaurs)

SIZE: About 40 feet (12 m) long, 12 feet (3.6 m) high at the hips

WEIGHT: About 6 tons

FRIENDS: None

ENEMIES: *Spinosaurus, Deltadromeus*

TRIVIA: *Carcharodontosaurus* teeth seem to be relatively common fossils in northern Africa.

*C*archarodontosaurus ("great-white-shark-tooth lizard") was first known only from its enormous teeth. When these teeth were first described in 1927, they were thought to come from a giant species of *Megalosaurus*. In 1931, however, paleontologists thought that they were different enough to be given their own name—after the great white shark, whose teeth this dinosaur's resembled.

When parts of this dinosaur's skeleton were finally discovered in northern Africa, they revealed a predator as big as *Tyrannosaurus rex*. Sadly, these fossils, kept in a museum in Munich, Germany, were destroyed by a bomb during World War II. But many decades later, in the summer of 1995, a team of paleontologists led by Paul Sereno found the most complete fossils yet of *Carcharodontosaurus*. These included most of the skull—including a braincase—as well as some other parts of the skeleton. This showed that *Carcharodontosaurus* was as big as the biggest *Tyrannosaurus*!

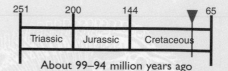

251	200	144	65
Triassic	Jurassic	Cretaceous	

About 99–94 million years ago

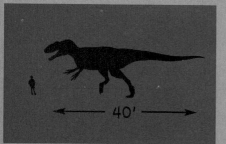

← 40' →

Comparison is with a 4-foot child

CARNOTAURUS
KAHR-no-TAWR-us

(year named: 1985)

Carnotaurus ("meat [-eating] bull") was one of the most bizarre meat-eating dinosaurs ever found. Its skull was short, with armor on the top and a pair of knobby horns over its eyes. The neck and shoulder blades were well developed, but the arms were incredibly short, with forearms so shrunken they were practically just wrists! Not even *Tyrannosaurus rex* had such small arms.

With its small skull, *Carnotaurus* might not have been able to attack big plant-eaters, but it was probably fast and could have easily chased down smaller, more agile prey.

The horns of *Carnotaurus* look something like those of a bull—and like a bull, it may have used them in contests with others of its own species. In this way, two *Carnotaurus* could test each other's strength without either of them seriously injuring the other.

FUN FACTS: The first, and so far only, discovered specimen of *Carnotaurus* was found with impressions of skin from all over the body.

LOCATION: Chubut Province, Argentina

FOOD: Other dinosaurs

SIZE: Almost 22 feet (6.5 m) long, 6.6 feet (2 m) high at the hips

WEIGHT: 1 ton

TRIVIA: In Michael Crichton's novel *The Lost World: Jurassic Park II*, the genetically re-created *Carnotaurus* had the power of chameleon-like camouflage. However, it is extremely unlikely that any dinosaur really had this ability.

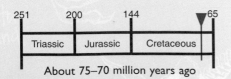

251	200	144	65
Triassic	Jurassic	Cretaceous	

About 75–70 million years ago

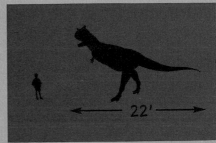

22'

Comparison is with a 4-foot child

CAUDIPTERYX

kaw-DIP-ter-iks

(year named: 1998)

FUN FACTS: Some *Caudipteryx* fossils have been found with stomach stones, which would have helped grind up their food.

LOCATION: Liaoning Province, China

FOOD: Possibly plants, small reptiles and mammals, eggs

SIZE: About 24 inches (61 cm) long, almost 20 inches (50 cm) high at the hips

WEIGHT: About 24 lbs (11 kg)

TRIVIA: One of the newest dinosaur museums in the world is being built in China next to the site where *Caudipteryx* and other feathered dinosaur fossils were found.

Caudipteryx ("tail feathers") was one of the most amazing dinosaur discoveries of the 20th century. It showed a dinosaur that was not a bird but had true feathers on its arms and tail.

Some scientists thought *Caudipteryx* was no more than some kind of primitive flightless bird, but when the skeleton of this little creature was studied in detail, it turned out to be an oviraptorosaur. Oviraptorosaurs were a type of meat-eating dinosaur common in the Late Cretaceous of Asia and North America. *Caudipteryx* was the oldest of the oviraptorosaurs and one of the most primitive.

The arms of *Caudipteryx* were very short, so it certainly could not fly. Then why did it have feathers? Paleontologists suggest a number of possibilities. It might be that they were used for signaling other *Caudipteryx*, as a peacock does. They might have been used to cover *Caudipteryx*'s eggs while it brooded its nest. Or possibly the ancestors of *Caudipteryx* really did fly but later become grounded (as happened with ostriches, kiwis, and chickens). We may never know for sure.

Comparison is with a 4-foot child

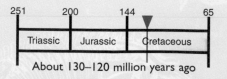

251	200	144		65
Triassic	Jurassic	Cretaceous		

About 130–120 million years ago

CENTROSAURUS
SEN-tro-SAWR-us

(year named: 1904)

In the 1800s, *Centrosaurus* ("spur lizard") was discovered in what is now called Dinosaur Provincial Park, in Alberta, Canada. This is one of the largest dinosaur graveyards in the world. In the 1980s, paleontologists discovered the "Centrosaurus Bonebed" within the park. The bonebed contains the skeletons of thousands of *Centrosaurus* that perished while crossing a river during a flood. This allows scientists a rare chance to see how *Centrosaurus* changed as it grew old.

Scientists had argued for years over whether *Centrosaurus* was the same animal as *Monoclonius*. The confusion resulted from the fact that horned dinosaurs' heads changed a lot as the animals grew older. Juveniles did not have the bumps, hooks, spikes, and knobs found on the skulls of adults. The dinosaur once known as *Monoclonius* is now regarded as a juvenile form of *Centrosaurus* and other horned dinosaurs.

FUN FACTS: One of the most common injuries in *Centrosaurus* skeletons is a broken tail. Apparently, it was quite common for them to get stepped on!

LOCATION: Alberta, Canada

FOOD: Conifers, cycads, ginkgos, flowering plants

SIZE: 20 feet (6 m) long, 6.6 feet (2 m) high at the hips

WEIGHT: 3 tons

TRIVIA: Dinosaur Provincial Park is a World Heritage Preserve. This means that the United Nations regards this park as a treasure for the whole world.

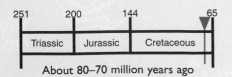

251	200	144	65
Triassic	Jurassic	Cretaceous	

About 80–70 million years ago

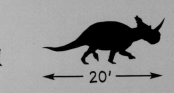

← 20' →

Comparison is with a 4-foot child

CERATOSAURUS

se-RAT-o-SAWR-us

(year named: 1884)

FUN FACTS: Although it was smaller overall than *Allosaurus*, *Ceratosaurus* had bigger teeth than its rival.

LOCATION: Colorado, Wyoming, Utah, Tanzania, Switzerland

FOOD: Other dinosaurs (sauropods, stegosaurs, ornithopods, smaller theropods)

SIZE: Almost 24 feet (7.2 m) long, over 6.2 feet (1.9 m) high at the hips

WEIGHT: Over 1 ton

TRIVIA: The horns on the nose and in front of the eyes of *Ceratosaurus* got bigger as the dinosaur got older.

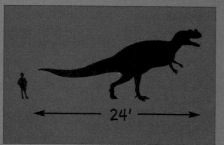

24'

Comparison is with a 4-foot child

Ceratosaurus ("horned lizard") was one of the first meat-eating dinosaurs known from a nearly complete skeleton. The first *Ceratosaurus* was found in 1883 in the Garden Park Quarry of Canyon City, Colorado. This area has produced many of the most important Jurassic fossils known. Although some parts of the arms and legs were missing, the rest of the skeleton was almost complete. Before this discovery, no skeleton of a large meat-eating dinosaur had been found that was more than half complete. These bones gave paleontologists many of their first insights into predatory dinosaurs.

Ceratosaurus was unusual for a meat-eater—it had a horn on its nose. The horn was very thin side-to-side (unlike the horns of the plant-eaters like *Centrosaurus* and *Triceratops*, which were cone-shaped). This horn, and the smaller horns just in front of its eyes, were very delicate and probably used only for signaling to other *Ceratosaurus*. The huge teeth and powerful jaws were probably *Centrosaurus*'s main weapons, since its arms and claws were small and feeble.

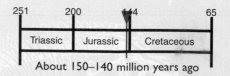

251	200	144	65
Triassic	Jurassic	Cretaceous	

About 150–140 million years ago

CHIROSTENOTES
KIE-ro-STEN-o-teez
(year named: 1924)

Chirostenotes ("slender hands") has had a confusing history. Different parts of this dinosaur were found separately at different times and given different names. The hands were found first, in 1924, and given the name *Chirostenotes*. Then the feet were found in 1932 and given the name *Macrophalangia* ("big toes"). Both the hands and feet were recognized (correctly) as being from a small meat-eating dinosaur, but paleontologists were not certain if it was the same species of dinosaur or not. In 1936, the toothless jaws were found and thought to be from a bird, *Caenagnathus* ("modern [style] jaws").

In 1988, a specimen that had been in storage since 1923 was studied. This fossil helped to join these different parts together because it showed that these types of jaws, feet, and hands were all from the same dinosaur! This fossil also showed that *Chirostenotes* was an oviraptorosaur, a relative of the Asian *Caudipteryx* and *Oviraptor*.

FUN FACTS: The Dinosaur Park Formation in Canada has produced more dinosaur species than any other Cretaceous formation.

LOCATION: Alberta, Canada

FOOD: Possibly small reptiles and mammals, plants, eggs, insects

SIZE: About 9.5 feet (2.9 m) long, about 3.1 feet (0.95 m) high at the hips

WEIGHT: About 110 lbs (50 kg)

TRIVIA: A set of jaws with unusual teeth were once thought to be from *Chirostenotes*. Now that we known that *Chirostenotes* had toothless jaws, these toothed fossils (now called *Ricardoestesia*) are from a mystery dinosaur!

251	200	144	65
Triassic	Jurassic	Cretaceous	

About 80–70 million years ago

55

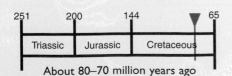

← 9.5' →

Comparison is with a 4-foot child

COELOPHYSIS
SEEL-o-FIE-sis
(year named: 1889)

FUN FACTS: *Coelophysis* is known from more skeletons than any other meat-eating dinosaur of the Mesozoic.
LOCATION: New Mexico, Arizona
FOOD: Small reptiles and fish
SIZE: 10 feet (3 m) long, 24 inches (60 cm) high at the hips
WEIGHT: 55 lbs (25 kg)
FRIENDS: None
ENEMIES: *Postosuchus* (a giant predatory crocodile relative)

Coelophysis ("hollow form") was one of the first meat-eating dinosaurs. When *Coelophysis* lived, dinosaurs had just evolved, and they did not yet dominate the land. Instead, giant relatives of crocodilians were the top predators, and armored crocodile relatives and ox-sized protomammals—primitive synapsids related to the ancestors of mammals—were the big plant-eaters. *Coelophysis* was a minor predator in its environment, but it was very successful. Unlike their crocodilian relatives, *Coelophysis* and other early dinosaurs were fast-running, agile hunters.

In 1947, hundreds of *Coelophysis* skeletons were found buried together at Ghost Ranch, New Mexico. This spectacular discovery included old

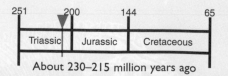

251	200	144	65
Triassic	Jurassic	Cretaceous	

About 230–215 million years ago

individuals, babies, and all ages in between. Except for a few other reptiles, the only skeletons in this quarry were from *Coelophysis*. This suggests that these early dinosaurs would group together, at least occasionally. Some paleontologists think that this mass death might have happened when a pack of *Coelophysis* gathered near a water hole and were buried by a flash flood. In the bellies of some of the *Coelophysis* were the skeletons of baby *Coelophysis*—it seems that they were eaten by the adults!

10'

Comparison is with a 4-foot child

57

COMPSOGNATHUS

komp-SOG-na-thus (KOMP-so-NAH-thus)

(year named: 1861)

FUN FACTS: *Compsognathus* was the first dinosaur known from a nearly complete fossil.
LOCATION: Germany and France
FOOD: Small reptiles and mammals, possibly insects
SIZE: 4 feet (1.1 m) long, 10 inches (26 cm) high at the hips
WEIGHT: 7.7 pounds (3.5 kg)
FRIENDS: None
ENEMIES: Bigger theropods

Compsognathus ("delicate jaw") was once considered the smallest known dinosaur. The first discovered fossil of *Compsognathus* was less than 28 inches (70 cm) long; however, this specimen was probably not fully grown. Even so, adult *Compsognathus* probably weighed only about 7.7 pounds (3.5 kg). Although scientists now regard birds as dinosaurs (and therefore, there are many living dinosaurs smaller than *Compsognathus*), this little meat-eater from the Jurassic Period of Europe is still one of the smallest dinosaurs known from the Mesozoic Era, the Age of Dinosaurs.

Inside the belly of the original *Compsognathus* specimen is the skeleton of a fast-running lizard. This shows that *Compsognathus* was a meat-eater like its bigger relatives (such as *Tyrannosaurus* and *Giganotosaurus*), but it hunted much smaller prey. It lived on the same tropical islands as *Archaeopteryx*, and perhaps it would even eat its smaller flying relative.

Compsognathus had short arms that were probably not very useful in catch-

Comparison is with a 4-foot child

ing prey, but that were handy for holding on to victims it snatched up in its jaws. For many years, it was thought that *Compsognathus* had only two fingers on each hand (as in *Tyrannosaurus* and other tyrant dinosaurs). However, it now seems that *Compsognathus* had three fingers on each hand like most meat-eaters.

Compsognathus seems to have been a close relative of the Chinese *Sinosauropteryx*, and like that Asian dinosaur it probably had a covering of "protofeathers." Unfortunately, neither protofeathers nor scales were preserved in the known fossils of *Compsognathus*.

TRIVIA: Only two skeletons of *Compsognathus* are presently known: one from Germany and a slightly larger one from France.
In *Jurassic Park II: The Lost World,* the genetically re-created *Compsognathus* ran around in packs, attacking much larger animals. While some smaller predators did hunt in packs, there is no evidence that the real *Compsognathus* did this.

TAKE TWO!
This scene taken from *The Lost World: Jurassic Park* shows a pack of *Compsognathus* attacking a member of the safari team.

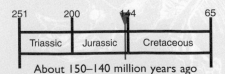

251	200	144	65
Triassic	Jurassic	Cretaceous	

About 150–140 million years ago

59

CONFUCIUSORNIS
kon-FYOO-shis-OR-nis

(year named: 1995)

FUN FACTS: *Confuciusornis* is known from so many fossils that it may be the most common Mesozoic dinosaur ever found.

LOCATION: Liaoning Province, China

FOOD: Possibly insects and plants

SIZE: 8 inches (20 cm) long, 4 inches (10 cm) tall, 14 inches (36 cm) wingspan

WEIGHT: 14 ounces (400 g)

TRIVIA: People have often tried to sell fake *Confuciusornis* skeletons. They sometimes give them extra leg bones or leave bones out!

onfuciusornis ("Confucius's bird") is one of the oldest and most primitive birds known. It is more advanced than *Archaeopteryx* because the bones at the end of its tail are fused into a single structure, as in modern birds. *Confuciusornis* is also the oldest known bird that had lost all of its teeth. This actually evolved independently of the loss of teeth in modern birds. In fact, Mesozoic toothed birds like *Hesperornis* are much more closely related to the birds of today than to *Confuciusornis*.

Confuciusornis comes from the spectacular Yixian Formation of China, so the feathers in most specimens are very well preserved. From this we see that some *Confuciusornis* had two long tail feathers, while most did not. Perhaps the ones with the long tail feathers were males, and the ones without were females.

Confuciusornis is known from hundreds of skeletons. Perhaps great flocks of *Confuciusornis* flew across the skies of Early Cretaceous China.

← 8" →

Comparison is with a 4-foot child

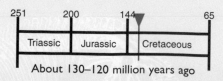

251	200	144	65
Triassic	Jurassic	Cretaceous	

About 130–120 million years ago

CORYTHOSAURUS

ko-RITH-o-SAWR-us

(year named: 1914)

Corythosaurus ("Corinthian helmet lizard") is one of the crested duckbill dinosaurs. At one time, over six species were named based on slight differences in the crest on the skull. But in 1975, paleontologist Peter Dodson showed that these changes are due to sexual dimorphism and growth allometry. In other words, they were all the same species, and the differences in the skulls and crests were normal among a large population of juveniles and adults of both sexes.

The famous crest of Corythosaurus is formed from the upper lip bone and the nasal bone. These two bones have grown back and up over the skull, taking the nasal passage with them. The result is a folded nasal passage comparable to a woodwind instrument, such as a clarinet. Each species of crested duckbill dinosaur would have made its own unique sound, like different instruments in an orchestra. The crest also housed the enlarged olfactory lobes of the brain, increasing the duckbill's sense of smell. In some species, the olfactory lobes are actually bent toward the hollow crest in order to be closer to the nasal chambers!

FUN FACTS: This was the first dinosaur found with an almost complete skin!

LOCATION: Alberta, Canada

FOOD: Conifers, cycads, ginkgos, angiosperms

SIZE: 33 feet (10 m) long, 6.6 feet (2 m) high at the hips

WEIGHT: 5 tons

TRIVIA: The most beautiful and complete Corythosaurus skeleton is on display at the American Museum of Natural History in New York City.

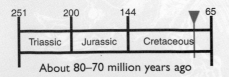

251	200	144		65
Triassic	Jurassic	Cretaceous		

About 80–70 million years ago

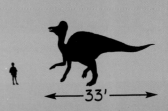

Comparison is with a 4-foot child

61

CRYOLOPHOSAURUS

krie-o-LOF-o-SAWR-us

(year named: 1994)

FUN FACTS: Other dinosaurs from Antarctica, presently unnamed, include ankylosaurs and duckbills from the Cretaceous Period.

LOCATION: Antarctica

FOOD: Other dinosaurs

SIZE: Perhaps 20 feet (6 m) long, perhaps 5 feet (1.5 m) high at the hips

WEIGHT: Perhaps 1,155 lbs (525 kg)

TRIVIA: Although *Cryolophosaurus* is the first named Mesozoic dinosaur from Antarctica, penguins are the best-known dinosaurs from the frozen land. (Remember: Birds are a kind of dinosaur and penguins are a kind of bird!)

Cryolophosaurus ("frozen-crested lizard") is the first fossil dinosaur from Antarctica that has been officially named. The only known fossil of this dinosaur was recovered from the Transantarctic Mountains in 1990. This is one of the few places in Antarctica where the rock sticks up through the glaciers. In most spots, the rocks (and fossils in them) are buried under a mile or more of ice.

Although a frozen land now, Antarctica was not always covered in ice. During the Age of Dinosaurs, the world was warmer in general, and Antarctica was farther north than it is today. All sorts of animals and plants once flourished there. It was only after the Age of Dinosaurs that Antarctica shifted over the South Pole and became buried in ice.

Cryolophosaurus was a meat-eating dinosaur and seems to have been a close relative of *Allosaurus*. Its most distinctive feature is its forward-facing crest. The remains of a prosauropod dinosaur were found with the skeleton of *Cryolophosaurus*, so it is likely that prosauropods were the prey of choice.

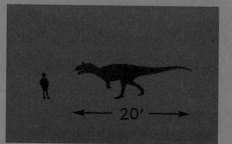

20'

Comparison is with a 4-foot child

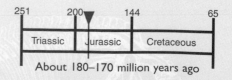

251	200	144	65
Triassic	Jurassic	Cretaceous	

About 180–170 million years ago

DEINONYCHUS
die-NON-i-kus
(year named: 1969)

Deinonychus ("terrible claw") is one of the most important dinosaurs ever found because it changed the way paleontologists thought about dinosaurs. For most of the 20th century, dinosaurs were generally thought of as being strange evolutionary "dead ends," with no living descendants, mostly slow and sluggish. Then dinosaur paleontogist Dr. John Ostrom discovered *Deinonychus* in 1964.

Dr. Ostrom believed that this dinosaur was an agile, swift predator, more like a warm-blooded mammal or bird than a cold-blooded crocodile. His study of *Deinonychus*—and of the early bird *Archaeopteryx*—led him to realize that birds were in fact the descendants of dinosaurs, and that raptor dinosaurs such as *Deinonychus* and *Velociraptor* were among the closest relatives of birds.

Deinonychus was the first of the raptors (technically called "dromaeosaurs") to be known from a nearly complete skeleton. *Velociraptor* had been discovered forty years earlier but was known only from a skull and a few bones of its hands and feet. The skeletons of *Deinonychus* were the first to show the now infamous sickle-shaped retractable foot claw, used for ripping open the guts of its prey.

FUN FACTS: *Deinonychus* had "terrible claws," but it *also* had a nasty bite, with over 60 knife-like teeth!

LOCATION: Montana, Wyoming, possibly Maryland

FOOD: Other dinosaurs

SIZE: Over 11 feet (3.4 m) long, 34 inches (87 cm) high at the hips

WEIGHT: Over 160 lbs (73 kg)

TRIVIA: The genetically recreated *Velociraptors* seen in the *Jurassic Park* movies are closer in size to a very large *Deinonychus* than to the true *Velociraptor*, which was much smaller.

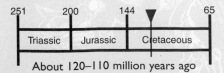

251	200	144		65
Triassic	Jurassic	Cretaceous		

About 120–110 million years ago

11'

Comparison is with a 4-foot child

63

DILOPHOSAURUS
die-LOF-o-SAWR-us
(year named: 1970)

Raptor foot

FUN FACTS: The state fossil of Connecticut is a dinosaur footprint, very likely the footprint of *Dilophosaurus* or a close relative.

LOCATION: Arizona, China

FOOD: Prosauropods, primitive bird-hipped dinosaurs

SIZE: Over 22 feet (6.8 m) long, 5 feet (1.5 m) high at the hips

WEIGHT: 880 lbs (400 kg)

TRIVIA: When the first skeleton of this dinosaur was found (in 1942), it was thought to be from a new species of *Megalosaurus*. Only later in the lab did paleontologist Sam Welles discover the pair of crests on its head.

Dilophosaurus ("double-crested lizard") was one of the first large meat-eating dinosaurs. It was a close relative of the smaller dinosaur *Coelophysis*. Little *Coelophysis* lived in the Late Triassic, when *Rauisuchus* and other reptiles related to the ancestors of crocodilians were the top predators. At the end of the Triassic, however, there was a series of great extinctions, and the giant crocodile relatives became extinct. Dinosaurs then became the top meat-eaters.

In general, *Dilophosaurus* looks like a shorter-necked, more heavily built version of *Coelophysis*. Like its little relative, *Dilophosaurus* has a characteristic "kink" in the front of its snout. This probably helped hold on to struggling victims. One dramatic difference (other than size) between the two is the pair of tall crescent-shaped crests along the top of *Dilophosaurus*'s skull. These were very thin and probably used only for display.

Footprints that match the feet of *Dilophosaurus* are found in many parts of the world, dating from Early Jurassic. Since the continents of the Earth were still mostly attached as the supercontinent of Pangaea at this time (see map on page 151), it is possible that the double-crested hunter lived in most parts of the world.

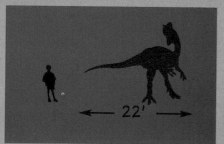

← 22' →

Comparison is with a 4-foot child

64

TAKE TWO!

The *Dilophosaurus* shown below is from the motion picture *Jurassic Park*. Note that the frill, the *T. rex*–like skull, and the poisonous spit were clearly the result of DNA splicing by InGen. There is no evidence that these features were present in the *Dilophosaurus* that lived during the Age of Dinosaurs.

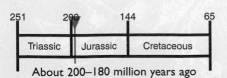

251   200   144   65

| Triassic | Jurassic | Cretaceous |

About 200–180 million years ago

DRYOSAURUS

DRIE-o-SAWR-us

(year named: 1878)

FUN FACTS: *Dryosaurus* could outrun a human.

LOCATION: Wyoming, Utah, Colorado, Tanzania

FOOD: conifers, cycads, ginkgos

SIZE: 9.5 feet (just under 3 m) long, 5 feet (1.7 m) high at the hips

WEIGHT: 200 pounds (91 kg)

FRIENDS: *Othnielia, Camptosaurus, Stegosaurus*

ENEMIES: *Coelurus, Ornitholestes, Allosaurus*

TRIVIA: The African species of *Dryosaurus* is named after General Lettow-Vorbeck , a German hero of World War I.

Dryosaurus ("oak-tree lizard") literally lived in the shadows of most Late Jurassic plants. It was a small to medium-sized dinosaur and was very lightly built (as compared to its closest relative, the bulkier *Camptosaurus*). *Dryosaurus* was one of the ornithopods, or beaked dinosaurs. Its pelvis is small compared to the rest of the body. The arms are very short and the long legs not powerfully built. The skull has a short face and relatively big eyes.

A dinosaur like *Dryosaurus* had to rely on running from predators (rather than standing and fighting), so it had to grow as fast as possible. The longer its legs, the faster it would run. Not all dinosaurs grew as fast as *Dryosaurus*. Modern lizards, for example, grow in spurts, depending on the season. But *Dryosaurus*'s bones grew fast at all times, which was a great benefit to its survival.

← 9.5' →

Comparison is with a 4-foot child

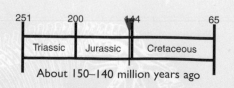

251	200	144	65
Triassic	Jurassic	Cretaceous	

About 150–140 million years ago

DRYPTOSAURUS

DRIP-to-SAWR-us

(year named: 1866)

Dryptosaurus ("tearing lizard") has an important place in the history of dinosaur science. Before this species was discovered in 1866, paleontologists had never found the arms *and* legs of the same species of a meat-eating dinosaur. Because of this, they thought that meat-eaters were four-legged hunters, like giant lizards or bears. However, when *Dryptosaurus* was found, scientists saw that meat-eating dinosaurs had arms that were much shorter than their legs, and realized they had to be bipedal, or two-footed.

Dryptosaurus was named for its enormous 8-inch (21-cm) claw. Its discoverer, Edward Drinker Cope, thought that this claw came from the foot, but it was later realized that this was actually a hand claw. Unfortunately, not much of the skeleton of *Dryptosaurus* was ever found. Paleontologists must guess at what it may have looked like.

FUN FACTS: A famous painting by artist Charles R. Knight shows two *Dryptosaurus* fighting, with one of them leaping high in the air to pounce on the other. This is an exciting image but an unlikely scenario for animals of their size!

LOCATION: New Jersey

FOOD: *Hadrosaurus*

SIZE: Perhaps 22 feet (6.5 m) long, 6 feet (1.8 m) high at the hips

WEIGHT: Perhaps 1.2 tons

FRIENDS: None

ENEMIES: None

TRIVIA: *Dryptosaurus* was first named *Laelaps*. It was then discovered that the name had already been used—for a type of tick!

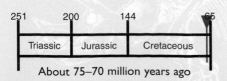

251	200	144	65
Triassic	Jurassic	Cretaceous	

About 75–70 million years ago

22'

Comparison is with a 4-foot child

EDMONTONIA

ED-mon-TOE-nee-uh

(year named: 1928)

FUN FACTS: *Edmontonia* had flexible body armor.

LOCATION: Montana; South Dakota; Wyoming; Alberta, Canada; possibly Alaska

FOOD: Conifers, cycads, ginkgos

SIZE: About 23 feet (just under 7 m) long, 6.6 feet (2 m) high at the hips

WEIGHT: 2.5 tons

TRIVIA: The best full-scale restoration is on display at the Royal Tyrrell Museum in Drumheller, Alberta, Canada.

E dmontonia ("lizard from Edmonton [Canada]") is a nodosaur, a kind of ankylosaur without a tail club. It had two large spikes on each shoulder that pointed out to the side. These spikes were a great defense against predators because they were at the same level as the knee and calf muscles of a larger theropod, or meat-eating dinosaur. If attacked, this slow-moving tank would throw its weight behind these spikes and drive them into a predator's legs. This would immediately disable the attacker and allow *Edmontonia* to walk away.

Although the skull of *Edmontonia* was long and shallow, it had room for four sinus cavities. This meant the skull was lighter, and probably improved the dinosaur's sense of smell. *Edmontonia*'s teeth were amazingly small for such a large animal. One tooth was only half an inch (1 cm) long and barely a fifth of an inch (5 mm) wide—far too small for eating most plants. Did *Edmontonia* also eat ants and insects, like the modern anteater? Or were its teeth disappearing over time because its beak did all the work? These are mysteries that dinosaur detectives have yet to solve!

23'

Comparison is with a 4-foot child

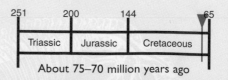

251	200	144	65
Triassic	Jurassic	Cretaceous	

About 75–70 million years ago

EINIOSAURUS
EYE-nee-o-SAWR-us
(year named: 1995)

Einiosaurus (Blackfoot Indian for "buffalo lizard") is one of the centrosaurine ceratopsians. Ceratopsians, or frilled dinosaurs, are divided into several groups. The first group to appear was the psittacosaurs. The second group was the protoceratopsians. The third group was the centrosaurines (with a single big horn over the nose). The last group was the chasmosaurines (with two big horns over the eyes).

Einiosaurus is easily recognized because it looks like a horned dinosaur with both a can opener and a bottle opener attached to its head! The nasal horn (or "can opener") is highly recurved—first up and forward, and then down. It has a wide base and is very narrow, much like certain types of war spears. The "bottle opener" is at the back of the frill. These two long prongs of bone would have protected the neck from attacks by tyrannosaurs.

FUN FACTS: *Einiosaurus* lived on the western shore of the ancient sea that is now the Rocky Mountains.
LOCATION: Montana
FOOD: Conifers, cycads, ginkgos, flowering plants
SIZE: 20 feet (6 m) long, 6.6 feet (2 m) high at the hips
WEIGHT: 2 tons
FRIENDS: *Achelousaurus, Styracosaurus*
ENEMIES: *Albertosaurus, Saurornitholestes*
TRIVIA: In 1996, *Einiosaurus* was featured on a U.S. postage stamp drawn by James Gurney.

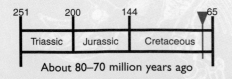

251	200	144	65
Triassic	Jurassic	Cretaceous	

About 80–70 million years ago

← 20' →

Comparison is with a 4-foot child

ELAPHROSAURUS
EL-a-fro-SAWR-us
(year named: 1920)

FUN FACTS: The only known skeleton of *Elaphrosaurus* on display is mounted with a skull based on that of a *Velociraptor*.

LOCATION: Tanzania, possibly western North America

FOOD: Small reptiles, including smaller dinosaurs

SIZE: Almost 20.5 feet (6.2 m) long, 5 feet (1.5 m) high at the hips

WEIGHT: About 460 lbs (210 kg)

TRIVIA: Based on the proportions of its very long legs, paleontologists think that *Elaphrosaurus* may have been the fastest dinosaur of the Jurassic Period.

Elaphrosaurus ("fleet lizard") was a meat-eating dinosaur with a long neck and tail and very long hind legs. Unfortunately, we don't know what its head looked like because the skull has never been found.

What scientists know of *Elaphrosaurus* comes from a nearly complete skeleton recovered from the Tendaguru Beds of Tanzania. These beds contain the best Late Jurassic Epoch dinosaur fossils in Africa. They are famous for the many skeletons of giant long-necked sauropods, plated stegosaurs, and beaked ornithopods that have been found there.

Unfortunately, paleontologists digging at Tendaguru have found very few fossils of theropods, or meat-eating dinosaurs. They have found teeth and bones and other bits, but the only nearly complete skeleton of a theropod found there was *Elaphrosaurus*.

Bones which *might* be from *Elaphrosaurus* (or a very closely related dinosaur) were found in the Morrison Formation, a famous series of rocks in western North America from the same time period as the Tendaguru Beds.

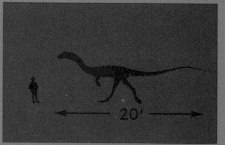

20'

Comparison is with a 4-foot child

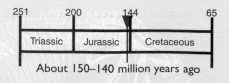

251	200	144	65
Triassic	Jurassic	Cretaceous	

About 150–140 million years ago

EORAPTOR
EE-o-RAP-tor
(year named: 1993)

Eoraptor ("dawn hunter") is the most primitive known dinosaur, and for paleontologists it serves as a model for what the very first dinosaur probably looked like.

Before *Eoraptor* was found, scientists looked at the oldest and most primitive members of each of the major groups of dinosaurs. They saw that most of these were only about 3.3 feet (1 m) long, and that they walked on their back legs. Then, in 1991, Ricardo Martinez found the skeleton of *Eoraptor* in Argentina. It matched what paleontologists had expected to find in a common ancestor. It was only 3.3 feet (1 m) long, and it walked on its back legs.

Was *Eoraptor* the ancestor of all dinosaurs?

Unfortunately, no. It lived too late in time. Other, more advanced dinosaurs were found in the same Late Triassic rocks where *Eoraptor* was found. But paleontologists haven't given up the search for that very first dinosaur. They are now searching for new fossils in even older rocks.

FUN FACTS: *Eoraptor* was found in the Valley of the Moon.

LOCATION: Argentina

FOOD: Small reptiles and mammals

SIZE: 3.3 feet (1 m) long, 15 inches (39 cm) high at the hips

WEIGHT: About 9.5 lbs (4.3 kg)

TRIVIA: When the thighbone of *Eoraptor* was first found, paleontologists at first thought it was a little crocodile relative. They realized that it was a dinosaur when the rest of the skeleton was dug up.

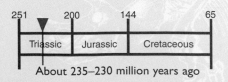

251	200	144	65
Triassic	Jurassic	Cretaceous	

About 235–230 million years ago

Comparison is with a 4-foot child

← 3.3' →

GALLIMIMUS

GAL-i-MIME-us

(year named: 1972)

Gallimimus ("chicken mimic") is one of the largest of the ornithomimosaurs (or "bird mimics"). Ornithomimosaurs are often called "ostrich dinosaurs" because they are shaped very similar to modern flightless birds.

Ostrich dinosaurs were compact, with long arms and legs. The arms ended in long hands with hook-like fingers all curling in the same direction. Their feet were long, narrow, and compact, and had a special shock-absorbing shape that let them run very fast. In fact, ostrich dinosaurs were probably the fastest dinosaurs of the Cretaceous Period. This would have been useful, since both raptors and tyrant dinosaurs hunted in the places where *Gallimimus* and its relatives lived!

Although *Pelecanimimus* and other early ostrich dinosaurs had teeth in their jaws, *Gallimimus* and its relatives were totally toothless. Their beaked heads had large eyes and were at the end of long, slender necks.

Some paleontologists think that ostrich dinosaurs ate only meat, although without good grasping hands or strong jaws they could kill only smaller animals. Others think that they were plant-eaters. Many suspect that like the modern ostrich, they ate small animals and plants.

FUN FACTS:

Gallimimus may not be the largest of all the ostrich dinosaurs. The arms and hands of *Deinocheirus* from Mongolia seem to be the size of *T. rex.*

LOCATION: Mongolia

FOOD: Possibly small mammals and reptiles, plants, insects

SIZE: 20 feet (6 m) long, 6.3 feet (1.9 m) high at the hips

WEIGHT: 968 lbs (440 kg)

TRIVIA: In *Jurassic Park*, *Gallimimus* is shown living in flocks. Paleontologists have not found skeletons of different *Gallimimus* together, but there are reports of such a discovery for an earlier Mongolian ostrich dinosaur.

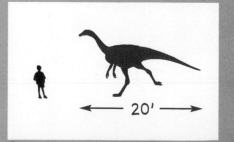

← 20' →

Comparison is with a 4-foot child

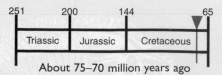

251	200	144	65
Triassic	Jurassic	Cretaceous	

About 75–70 million years ago

72

GARGOYLEOSAURUS
gahr-GOI-lee-o-SAWR-us
(year named: 1998)

Gargoylcosaurus ("gargoyle lizard") is one of the rarest of the armored dinosaurs. It is from the Jurassic Period, not the Cretaceous like most ankylosaurs. It has many primitive features. For example, in most ankylosaurs, the upper part of the beak has no teeth. The more teeth present in the beak, the more primitive the dinosaur. *Gargoyleosaurus* has seven teeth, more than in any other ankylosaur. Most ankylosaurs also have a set of large, folded nasal air passages. In *Gargoyleosaurus*, the small nasal air passage is straight. The most highly armored ankylosaurs have solid plates of bone (armor) on the outside of the body. In *Gargoyleosaurus*, they are hollow.

Ankylosaurs and stegosaurs are classified together in a larger group called the Thyreophora, or "armored dinosaurs." They share the common feature known as "dermal armor," or armor that grows out of the skin.

FUN FACTS: The armor of *Gargoyleosaurus* looks amazingly like the painted and spiked fans at an Oakland Raiders football game!

LOCATION: Wyoming

FOOD: Conifers, cycads, ginkgos

SIZE: 10 feet (3 m) long, 3.3 feet (1 m) high at the hips

WEIGHT: 1 ton

FRIENDS: *Stegosaurus, Othnielia, Mymoorapelta*

ENEMIES: *Ornitholestes, Torvosaurus*

TRIVIA: The only *Gargoyleosaurus* skull and skeleton on display are in the Denver Museum of Natural History.

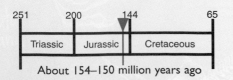

251	200	144	65
Triassic	Jurassic	Cretaceous	

About 154–150 million years ago

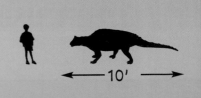

10'

Comparison is with a 4-foot child

73

GASPARINISAURA

gas-pah-REEN-ee-SAWR-a

(year named: 1996)

FUN FACTS: Of the many groups of ornithopods, only *Gasparinisaura* and the hadrosaurs are known from South America.

LOCATION: Patagonia, Argentina

FOOD: Conifers, cycads, ginkgos, possibly early weedlike flowering plants

SIZE: 2.5 feet (.8 m) long, 1 foot (.3 m) high at the hips

WEIGHT: 75 pounds (34 kg)

TRIVIA: The scientists who are studying the very small *Gasparinisaura* are the same scientists at work on the very large *Giganotosaurus*.

*G*asparinisaura ("[Dr. Zulma B.] Gasparini's lizard") is one of the rare ornithopods, or beaked dinosaurs, from the middle of the Cretaceous Period. Remains of dinosaurs from this time span are so extremely rare, all the specimens in the world would fit in one small exhibit hall!

Gasparinisaura is also one of those rare small dinosaurs that had a primitive body design. The features of its skeleton place it with the dryosaurs, from the Jurassic Period, but *Gasparinisaura* lived well into the Cretaceous Period—a time when the hadrosaurs, the most evolved of the ornithopods, had already appeared. Many features of the skull are primitive: for example, the teeth with low crowns (not much showing above the gum line) and the shortened face (later ornithopods have a long muzzle). Normally, the skull evolves faster than the body bones. But in *Gasparinisaura,* the reverse has occurred. The hip bone is more like that of the later hadrosaurs. This indicates a dinosaur with a well-developed hip musculature.

← 2.5' →

Comparison is with a 4-foot child

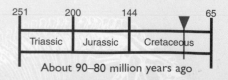

251	200	144	65
Triassic	Jurassic	Cretaceous	

About 90–80 million years ago

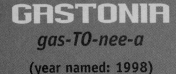

GASTONIA
gas-TO-nee-a
(year named: 1998)

Gastonia ("[Robert] Gaston's lizard") is a small, armored dinosaur with large, curved spikes projecting out of its back and along both sides of its body. The tail has sideways-aiming spikes along the sides. *Gastonia* was one of the most highly ornamented of all the ankylosaurs, or tank dinosaurs. Although it has an armored shield over the pelvis like the polacanthid ankylosaurs of Europe, it also has spiked armor, more like the nodosaurid ankylosaurs of North America.

Gastonia shares one major feature with most other later ankylosaurs. It has very short, powerful legs. This means that *Gastonia* could not outrun a predator but would stand and fight (which explains the fancy armor). Since *Gastonia* had spikes from the shoulder to the tip of the tail, plus a large shield of bone over the hips, there was no good place for a meat-eater to take a bite!

FUN FACTS: The original specimen is in the collections at the College of Eastern Utah in Price, Utah.
LOCATION: Utah
FOOD: Conifers, cycads, ginkgos
SIZE: 20 feet (6 m) long, almost 6.6 feet (2 m) high at the hips
WEIGHT: 1.5 tons
FRIENDS: Other small ankylosaurs
ENEMIES: *Utahraptor*
TRIVIA: The species name (*Gastonia burgei*) honors Don Burge, a dinosaur hunter from Utah.

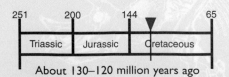

251	200	144		65
Triassic	Jurassic	Cretaceous		

About 130–120 million years ago

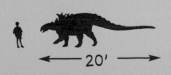

20'

Comparison is with a 4-foot child

GIGANOTOSAURUS

jig-a-NOT-o-SAWR-us

(year named: 1995)

Giganotosaurus ("giant southern lizard") is currently the

FUN FACTS: A cast of the skeleton of *Giganotosaurus* is on display at the Academy of Natural Sciences in Philadelphia, and

another will be put on display at the Fernbank Museum in Atlanta in the near future.

LOCATION: Argentina

FOOD: Titanosaurs and other sauropods

SIZE: Almost 43 feet (13 m) long, 13 feet (3.9 m) high at the hips

WEIGHT: About 8 tons

largest known meat-eating dinosaur ever. For many years *Tyrannosaurus* held that record (although bits and pieces of *Carcharodontosaurus* and *Spinosaurus* showed that they were as large as any individual *T. rex*). Then, in 1995, paleontologists Rodolfo Coria and Leonardo Salgado reported the discovery of a new meat-eater bigger than *any* tyrant dinosaur.

They named this dinosaur *Giganotosaurus*. Bone for bone, it was larger than the largest skeleton of *T. rex* ever found! The skull alone was 6 feet (1.8 m) long! What's more, a lower jawbone was later found from an individual even bigger than the first one—with a

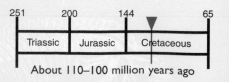

251	200	144	65
Triassic	Jurassic	Cretaceous	

About 110–100 million years ago

skull perhaps 6.5 feet (2 m) long. Clearly, *Giganotosaurus* was a gigantic dinosaur.

When *Giganotosaurus* was alive, the most common plant-eaters in South America were the titanosaur sauropods. While a single *Giganotosaurus* could kill a young titanosaur, it would take many *Giganotosaurus* to bring down a giant adult. At present, there is no evidence that *Giganotosaurus* hunted in groups, but a recent discovery from slightly younger rocks shows that the as-yet-unnamed descendant of *Giganotosaurus* may have lived in packs.

TRIVIA: *Giganotosaurus* might be the dinosaur whose name is most often misspelled and/or mispronounced. People often call it *Gigantosaurus* (with only one "o") instead of the proper *Giganotosaurus,* with two. The name *Gigantosaurus* was actually given to bits and pieces of a British long-necked sauropod dinosaur back in 1869.

Comparison is with a 4-foot child

GORGOSAURUS
GOR-go-SAWR-us
(year named: 1914)

FUN FACTS: *Gorgosaurus* was once considered a species of *Albertosaurus*, which is really a different (but closely related) tyrant dinosaur from later in the Cretaceous.

LOCATION: Alberta, Canada

FOOD: *Centrosaurus, Styracosaurus, Lambeosaurus, Corythosaurus, Euoplocephalus, Edmontonia*

SIZE: Over 28 feet (8.6 m) long, 9.3 feet (2.8 m) high at the hips

Gorgosaurus ("fierce lizard") was a tyrannosaur, or tyrant dinosaur. It was a very close relative of *Tyrannosaurus*—although *Gorgosaurus* was a little smaller and lived somewhat earlier.

The tyrant dinosaurs were very specialized meat-eaters. Their arms were extremely short, and they had only two fingers (the thumb and the index finger). The arms of *Gorgosaurus*—like those of *Tyrannosaurus*—were so short they couldn't even reach its mouth!

Tyrant dinosaurs' legs were long and slender, and their narrow, compact feet had a special shock-absorbing shape. A young *Gorgosaurus* was probably as fast as an ostrich dinosaur, and even an adult was probably faster than any of the duckbills and horned dinosaurs it hunted. Although its arms would be useless in catching prey, it could use its powerful jaws, filled with

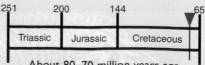

251	200	144	65
Triassic	Jurassic	Cretaceous	

About 80–70 million years ago

many strong teeth, to grab its victims. Tyrant dinosaurs' teeth, unlike those of most theropods, or meat-eating dinosaurs, were not shaped like blades. Instead, they were thick and round in cross-section. This meant that the teeth could be used to hold and grip tighter, and maybe even to crush bone.

When tyrant dinosaurs were around, they were the largest predators in their environment. The only meat-eater a *Gorgosaurus* had to fear was another *Gorgosaurus,* or the even larger tyrant dinosaur *Daspletosaurus,* which lived at the same time. Of course, *Gorgosaurus* would have to be careful when attacking a *Centrosaurus* or other horned dinosaur. Although these ceratopsians ate plants, they could still defend themselves with their deadly horns.

WEIGHT: 2.5 tons
FRIENDS: None
ENEMIES: *Daspletosaurus*
TRIVIA: Almost every dinosaur labeled *"Albertosaurus"* in a museum is really a *Gorgosaurus!*

28'

Comparison is with a 4-foot child

GRYPOSAURUS
GRIP-o-SAWR-us
(year named: 1914)

FUN FACTS: *Gryposaurus* belongs to the "Roman-nose" group of hadrosaurs (duckbills).

LOCATION: Montana, Canada, possibly New Jersey and South America

FOOD: Flowering plants like magnolias and cycads

SIZE: 28 feet (8.4 m) long, 7 feet (2.1 m) high at the hips

WEIGHT: 3.5 tons

TRIVIA: When a new duckbill was found in the mid-1990s in Argentina, it was placed back in *Kritosaurus*! What a mess!

G*ryposaurus* ("hook-nosed lizard") is a duckbill dinosaur known from several complete skeletons and skulls. Nevertheless, its relationship with other duckbills is shrouded in mystery. In the 1850s, a partial duckbill was discovered in New Jersey. It was named *Hadrosaurus*. In 1910, another, more complete duckbill was found in New Mexico. It was named *Kritosaurus*. Although *Hadrosaurus* lacked a skull, the body looked just like *Kritosaurus*. Then in 1914, the first complete duckbill was found in Alberta, Canada. It had an excellent skull and was named *Gryposaurus*.

Some scientists considered *Gryposaurus* and *Kritosaurus* to be the same creature. Priority went to the name *Kritosaurus* because it was named first.

Enter Jack Horner (the inspiration for the Dr. Grant character in *Jurassic Park*) in the early 1990s. Horner believed that only *Gryposaurus* was complete enough to have a valid name, and he confined the name *Kritosaurus* to the skeleton in New Mexico.

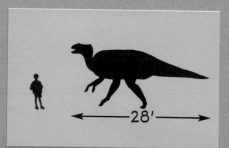

← 28' →

Comparison is with a 4-foot child

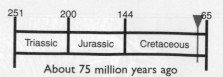

251	200	144	65
Triassic	Jurassic	Cretaceous	

About 75 million years ago

HADROSAURUS

HAD-ro-SAWR-us

(year named: 1854)

Hadrosaurus ("sturdy lizard") was—in the 1860s—the first dinosaur skeleton to be exhibited in North America. Its skeleton proved the theory that some dinosaurs walked on two legs, and not on all fours, as scientists of the time had thought. This dinosaur is poorly known because, to date, no skull has ever been found for it and no new skeletons have been found.

Older books may show you a head on this dinosaur, but those drawings are a guess on the part of the illustrators. At one time, scientists believed they had found the skull of Hadrosaurus, but it turned out to be the skull of another duckbill dinosaur, its closest relative, called Gryposaurus.

FUN FACTS: *Hadrosaurus* has its own Web site, www.levins.com/dinosaur.html
LOCATION: New Jersey
FOOD: Flowering plants, conifers, cycads, ginkgos
SIZE: 26 feet (8 m) long, about 6.6 feet (2 m) high at the hips
WEIGHT: 3 tons
FRIENDS: Other duckbills and ceratopsians, or horned dinosaurs
ENEMIES: Theropods, or meat-eaters, of any size
TRIVIA: The only *Hadrosaurus* specimen on exhibit in the world is at the Academy of Natural Sciences in Philadelphia.

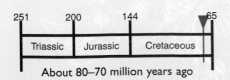

251	200	144

Triassic	Jurassic	Cretaceous

About 80–70 million years ago

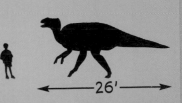

Comparison is with a 4-foot child

81

HERRERASAURUS

he-RER-a-SAWR-us

(year named: 1963)

FUN FACTS: One of the most complete mounted skeletons of *Herrerasaurus* can be seen at the Field Museum of Natural History in Chicago.

LOCATION: Argentina

FOOD: *Eoraptor* and prosauropods, and primitive bird-hipped dinosaurs

SIZE: Almost 13 feet (3.9 m) long, 4 feet (1.1 m) high at the hips

WEIGHT: 460 lbs (210 kg)

FRIENDS: None

ENEMIES: *Saurosuchus* (a giant crocodile relative)

TRIVIA: Before the first skull was discovered in 1988, *Herrerasaurus* was thought to be a prosauropod, an early form of the giant long-necked plant-eaters, like *Plateosaurus*.

Herrerasaurus ("[Victorino] Herrera's lizard") was one of the oldest and most primitive theropods, or meat-eating dinosaurs. And its body displayed many of the same features of the later theropods. It walked on its two hind legs, and its arms ended in powerful clawed hands for grasping prey. Its teeth—like those of most theropods—were shaped like blades and had knife-like serrations running up the front and down the back. Its lower jaw had a special hinge about halfway along its length. This joint would have helped *Herrerasaurus* to better hold on to struggling victims. Many later theropods also had this hinge.

Although *Herrerasaurus* shared the basic body design of future rulers of the Earth (like *Allosaurus*, *Giganotosaurus*, and *Tyrannosaurus*), it lived at a time when dinosaurs were *not* the most powerful predators. *Herrerasaurus* would have had to run away from the much larger *Saurosuchus*, a giant land-dwelling crocodile relative, which was the largest meat-eater in Argentina during the beginning of the Age of Dinosaurs.

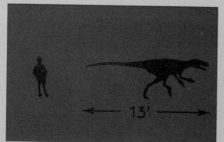

Comparison is with a 4-foot child

13'

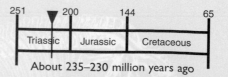

251	200	144	65
Triassic	Jurassic	Cretaceous	

About 235–230 million years ago

HESPERORNIS

HES-pe-ROR-nis

(year named: 1872)

Hesperornis ("western bird") was a flightless swimming bird with teeth. This may sound like a strange combination, but it is less weird than it seems. After all, there are flightless swimming birds today, such as the various species of penguin or the flightless cormorant of the Galápagos Islands.

Birds and raptors are closely related to each other, and both types of dinosaurs diverged from a common ancestor during the Jurassic. Birds evolved the ability to fly, and most birds of the Cretaceous were fliers. The ancestors of Hesperornis, however, became swimmers that chased fish. As time went by, the wings of this group of birds became shorter and shorter, until nothing remained of each wing but a simple spike. Hesperornis swam by using its feet to push itself quickly through the water, chasing after fish and squid. Its legs were so far back on its body that it probably had problems moving on land. However, like modern penguins, Hesperornis almost certainly came up onto land to lay its eggs.

FUN FACTS: During the Late Cretaceous, most of the middle of North America was covered by a shallow tropical sea. You could have taken a boat and sailed from the Gulf of Mexico to the Arctic Ocean over lands that are now prairies!

LOCATION: Kansas

FOOD: Fish, squid

SIZE: About 5 feet (1.5 m) long

WEIGHT: About 132 lbs (60 kg)

TRIVIA: Because birds are now classified as a kind of dinosaur, Hesperornis is technically a swimming dinosaur. Therefore, older books that say no dinosaurs lived in the sea are incorrect.

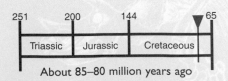

251	200	144	65
Triassic	Jurassic	Cretaceous	

About 85–80 million years ago

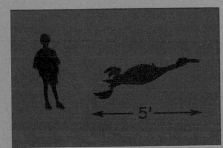

←— 5' —→

Comparison is with a 4-foot child

HETERODONTOSAURUS

HET-eh-ro-DON-to-SAWR-us

(year named: 1962)

FUN FACTS: This small dinosaur could have outrun a ten-year-old human.

LOCATION: Cape Province, South Africa

FOOD: Conifers, cycads, ginkgos, possibly insects

SIZE: Just over 3.3 feet (1 m) long and about 19 inches (less than .5 m) high at the hips

WEIGHT: 100 pounds (45 kg)

FRIENDS: Other early ornithopods

ENEMIES: Juvenile theropods, crocodiles

TRIVIA: A copy of the original skeleton can be seen at the Smithsonian Institution in Washington, D.C.

Heterodontosaurus ("different-tooth lizard") was a small, fast dinosaur with strong, grasping hands, long arms, and a powerful bite. These features are, for the most part, unnecessary in a plant-eater. It does not take speed, agility, and dexterity to overpower a leaf! Heterodontosaurus's most notable feature, however, is the set of "fangs" at the front of its mouth. It is quite unusual for a plant-eating dinosaur to have teeth like this, which you'd normally expect in a meat-eater.

We know of only one other Early Jurassic group of dinosaurs—the prosauropods—where some of its members had teeth structurally intermediate between those of meat-eaters and of plant-eaters. The same may be true here. Heterodontosaurus and prosauropods both might be examples of the transition from meat-eater to plant-eater.

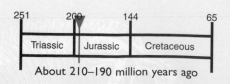

← 3' →

Comparison is with a 4-foot child

251	200	144	65
Triassic	Jurassic	Cretaceous	

About 210–190 million years ago

HOMALOCEPHALE and PRENOCEPHALE

ho-mal-o-SEF-a-lee　　*PREEN-o-SEF-a-lee*

(year named: 1974)

Homalocephale

Homalocephale ("even-headed lizard") and *Prenocephale* ("inclined head") are representatives of the Pachycephalosauria, or thick-headed dinosaurs, the last of the seven major groups of dinosaurs to appear, and the rarest. Some scientists divide pachycephalosaurs into two groups: flat heads and big-dome heads. *Homalocephale* is a flat head and *Prenocephale* is a big-dome head. In all cases, the skull and dome are composed of the same skull bones that are found in humans (the frontal and parietal bones). The edge of the pachycephalosaur's dome may include bumps, knobs, and, in some forms, spikes. Early pachycephalosaurs had small domes, which got progressively bigger over time. The largest dome can be found in *Pachycephalosaurus*.

Both dinosaurs are known from unusually complete skeletons. They were found in Mongolia—in an area supposedly barren of fossils!

FUN FACTS: These dinosaurs may have been the ecological equivalent of today's goats because of their small mouths and ability to eat anything without being picky.

LOCATION: Mongolia

FOOD: Plants

SIZE: About 5 feet (over 1 m) long and 3 feet (less than 1 m) high at the hips

WEIGHT: 350 pounds (159 kg)

TRIVIA: You can read an account of the amazing expedition that uncovered the fossils of these dinosaurs in *Hunting for Dinosaurs* by Zofia Kielan-Jaworowska.

Prenocephale

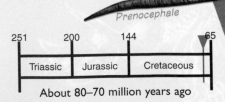

251	200	144	65
Triassic	Jurassic	Cretaceous	

About 80–70 million years ago

IGUANODON

ih-GWAHN-o-don

(year named: 1825)

FUN FACTS: Most *Iguanodon* skeletons are exhibited in the "old style," with the tail dragging on the ground. We now know that dinosaurs did not drag their tails.

LOCATION: Western Europe, mostly England and Belgium

FOOD: Conifers, cycads, ginkgos

SIZE: About 35 feet (11 m) long, 9 feet (2.7 m) high at the hips

WEIGHT: 5 tons

TRIVIA: The owners of the coal mine in Belgium shut it down for two years so that scientists could excavate the bones—a very rare case of cooperation between scientists and corporate land owners!

guanodon ("iguana tooth") was the first really huge ornithopod, or two-legged plant-eating dinosaur. The arms were longer than an adult human's, and all the bones of the skeleton were thick. This was a very powerful dinosaur that could defend itself quite well. Its massive arms ended in large hands that carried "thumb spikes." These were the perfect weapons to put out the eye of an attacking theropod.

Iguanodon is one of the original three members of the group Dinosauria. When Richard Owen coined the word *dinosaur* in 1842, he defined it to mean "fearfully great, a lizard." He based the name on three dinosaurs—*Megalosaurus*, *Iguanodon*, and *Hylaeosaurus*. The story of the discovery and naming of *Iguanodon* has been the subject of several books. No other two-footed plant-eater is as historically famous. One reason for this was a spectacular find in Bernissart, Belgium, in 1878. Workers in a coal mine found over a dozen well-preserved skeletons at a depth of over 1,000 feet (300 m).

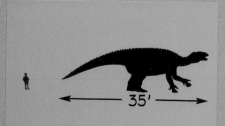

35'

Comparison is with a 4-foot child

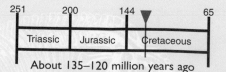

251	200	144		65
Triassic	Jurassic	Cretaceous		

About 135–120 million years ago

86

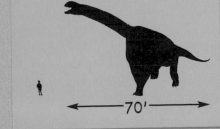

JOBARIA
jo-BAHR-ee-uh
(year named: 1999)

Jobaria (after a creature from Tuareg mythology) is a unique sauropod, or large long-necked dinosaur. It has thick, heavy legs and a very wide stance. Its teeth are thick and heavy, too. *Jobaria*'s neck is short, and so is the tail. This is a very powerful dinosaur. It fed mostly on the leaves of trees, so it had to be big enough to reach them, and big enough to support its own weight. *Jobaria* also had to fight off *Afrovenator* (the "*Allosaurus*" of this time) with its thumb claw!

Jobaria was found in 1997 but not named until 1999. Skeletons of several other specimens of *Jobaria* were unearthed at the same time, so it took years for the material to be prepared. Without the help of laboratory technicians who prepare the bones, scientists would need decades to describe and prepare new finds by themselves.

Imagine finding a dinosaur in the field. It has over 200 bones, many up to 6 feet (1.8 m) long and weighing several hundred pounds. You are working in a desert. The daily temperature is over 100 degrees, and the wind blasts sand in your face, clothes, and food. The nearest English-speaking country is over 1,000 miles (1,600 km) away! That's what Paul Sereno and his University of Chicago crew had to deal with while digging in the Sahara Desert for *Jobaria*.

FUN FACTS: *Jobaria* has its own Web page at www.jobaria.org.
LOCATION: Niger
FOOD: Conifers, cycads, ginkgos
SIZE: 70 feet (21 m) long, 15 feet (4.5 m) high at the hips
WEIGHT: 18 tons
FRIENDS: Other titanosaurs
ENEMIES: *Afrovenator*
TRIVIA: Casts of *Jobaria* are on display in Chicago.

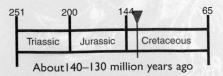

251	200	144	65
Triassic	Jurassic	Cretaceous	

About 140–130 million years ago

←—— 70' ——→

Comparison is with a 4-foot child

87

KENTROSAURUS
KEN-tro-SAWR-us

(year named: 1915)

FUN FACTS: The stegosaurs are the second rarest major group of dinosaurs. (The first are the pachycephalosaurs.)
LOCATION: Tanzania
FOOD: Conifers, cycads, ginkgos
SIZE: 18 feet (5.5 m) long, 5 feet (1.5 m) high at the hips
WEIGHT: 1 ton
FRIENDS: *Dryosaurus, Tornieria, Dicraeosaurus*
ENEMIES: *Elaphrosaurus,* possibly *Allosaurus, Ceratosaurus*
TRIVIA: The Humboldt Museum in Germany has the only mounted skeleton on display.

Kentrosaurus ("spiked lizard") is well named. A member of the Stegosauria, it has large spikes from the middle of its back down to the base of its tail. When compared to the North American *Stegosaurus*, *Kentrosaurus* has smaller plates. It appears that spikes evolved first in the Stegosauria, then plates developed from the spikes.

The bases of *Kentrosaurus*'s tail spikes are large and rounded, showing that they were solidly planted into the skin. This means that the spikes could not be waved independently in the direction of an attacker. There is also another shoulder spike that has been restored at times as facing both forward and backward. A backward-facing spike is more logical, however. With a forward-facing spike, *Kentrosaurus* might have impaled itself in the neck!

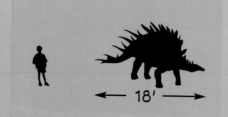

← 18' →

Comparison is with a 4-foot child

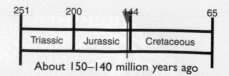

251	200	144	65
Triassic	Jurassic	Cretaceous	

About 150–140 million years ago

LEPTOCERATOPS
LEP-to-SAIR-ah-tops

(year named: 1914)

Leptoceratops ("slender horned face") had a head that was relatively large for its stocky body. This may mean that it never grew big, or that we have only found fossils of juveniles. *Leptoceratops* had only one defense, its parrot-like beak. The jaws of horned dinosaurs like *Leptoceratops* were the most powerful for their size of any plant-eater's. They had enough power, for example, to break the arm of any similar-sized theropod.

Leptoceratops is most similar to the earlier *Psittacosaurus* and *Protoceratops*. But *Leptoceratops* lived over 30 million years later, at the very end of the Age of Dinosaurs in North America. There are two possible explanations for this. The first is that *Leptoceratops*, or its ancestors, immigrated across the land bridge between Asia and North America at the end of the Cretaceous, but their fossils have so far been found only in North America. The second is that they were an early group of immigrants that survived only in North America, while their Asian ancestors went extinct.

FUN FACTS: *Leptoceratops* was named by Barnum Brown, the same man who found *Tyrannosaurus rex*.

LOCATION: Wyoming and Alberta, Canada

FOOD: Ground cover such as cycads and flowering plants

SIZE: 6.6 feet (2 m) long, 2.5 feet (.75 m) high at the hips

WEIGHT: 150 pounds (68 kg)

FRIENDS: *Edmontosaurus*, *Thescelosaurus*

ENEMIES: *Troodon*, juvenile tyrannosaurids

TRIVIA: The best display of *Leptoceratops* fossils is at the Museum of Nature in Ottawa, Canada.

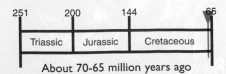

251	200	144	65
Triassic	Jurassic	Cretaceous	

About 70-65 million years ago

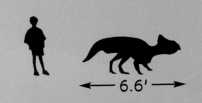

← 6.6' →

Comparison is with a 4-foot child

MAJUNGATHOLUS

mah-JOONG-gah-THOL-us

(year named: 1979)

FUN FACTS: The first pieces of *Majungatholus* found—some teeth and a jawbone—were thought to be from *Megalosaurus*.

LOCATION: Madagascar

FOOD: Titanosaurs

SIZE: About 26.4 feet (8 m) long, 7.9 feet (2.4 m) high at the hips

WEIGHT: About 1.9 tons

FRIENDS: None

ENEMIES: None

TRIVIA: For most of the Mesozoic, what is now the island of Madagascar was connected to India.

Majungatholus ("Majunga dome") was, until recently, a very poorly understood dinosaur. Bits and pieces of it have been found since 1896. In 1979, paleontologists described a piece of the top of the head of this dinosaur. Because it was so thick, and was covered by a knob of bone, they thought it was some kind of plant-eating pachycephalosaur.

In 1996, an expedition in Madagascar found the first good *Majungatholus* skull. It turned out that the thick dome and knob belonged not to a plant-eating pachycephalosaur but to a meat-eater! In fact, *Majungatholus* was a close relative to *Abelisaurus* and *Carnotaurus* (who also had thick skull roofs, although not as thick as that of *Majungatholus*).

Like *Carnotaurus*, *Majungatholus* had a fairly short skull with small teeth. It probably could not kill extremely large animals but could easily hunt down young ones. Also, like most theropods, or meat-eating dinosaurs, *Majungatholus* would almost certainly have scavenged a dinosaur corpse if it found one.

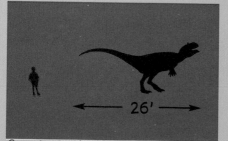

← 26' →

Comparison is with a 4-foot child

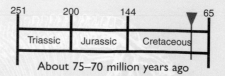

251	200	144	65
Triassic	Jurassic	Cretaceous	

About 75–70 million years ago

MAMENCHISAURUS
mah-MEN-chee-SAWR-us

(year named: 1954)

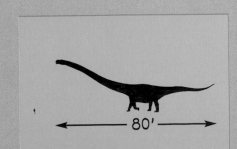

Mamenchisaurus ("lizard from Mamen's Brook") is basically a giant neck attached to a small body. The neck is about 40 feet (12 m) long, and the body is about the same length! The purpose of this short, wide body is to act as a stable, heavy base to anchor the neck. At the end of the neck is a short head with thick teeth. Its length allowed *Mamenchisaurus* to eat the leafy parts at the tops of some Jurassic trees. By doing so, it did not have to compete with its own young, who had to eat plants closer to the ground.

Functionally, this dinosaur could be called a "plant vacuum." Its super-long neck allowed it to suck up hundreds of pounds of leaves from treetops. Structurally, the neck represents the pinnacle of animal engineering. The vertebrae have hollow portions where there is little internal stress on the bones. This lightens the bones and makes them stronger. Struts and braces give added strength for load bearing. On top of the neck vertebrae are split spines that form a V-shaped trough. Inside this trough lies a series of ligaments that function like the cables on suspension bridges, holding up the neck.

FUN FACTS: This dinosaur had the longest neck in the history of Earth.
LOCATION: China
FOOD: Conifers, cycads, ginkgos
SIZE: About 80 feet (24 m) long, 15 feet (4.5 m) high at the hips
WEIGHT: 20 tons
FRIENDS: *Omeisaurus, Tuojiangosaurus, Chungkingosaurus*
ENEMIES: *Szechuanosaurus, Yangchuanosaurus*
TRIVIA: In *The Lost World: Jurassic Park*, did the guy on the motorcycle drive between the legs of a *Mamenchisaurus* or a *Diplodocus*?

Answer: In the book by Michael Crichton, it is a *Diplodocus*, but in the movie it looks more like a *Mamenchisaurus*.

251	200	▼ 144	65
Triassic	Jurassic	Cretaceous	

About 170–160 million years ago

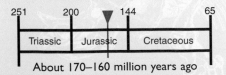

← 80' →

Comparison is with a 4-foot child

MASSOSPONDYLUS
mas-o-SPON-di-lus

(year named: 1854)

Raptor foot

FUN FACTS: Only the meat-eating theropods had bigger claws than prosauropods.
LOCATION: South Africa, Zimbabwe, Arizona
FOOD: Conifers, cycads, ginkgos
SIZE: About 19 feet (5.7 m) long, 6 feet (1.8 m) high at the hips
WEIGHT: 1.5 tons
FRIENDS: *Heterodontosaurus, Lycorhinus*
ENEMIES: *Syntarsus*
TRIVIA: *Massospondylus* could be the first dinosaur to claim the nickname "Claws." The first meat-eaters to have a claw that size did not appear until tens of millions of years later.

Massospondylus ("bulky vertebra") is a long, sleek plant-eating dinosaur with a huge claw on each hand. Theropods during the Early Jurassic had not yet reached "super size" (like *Allosaurus*), so a claw of this type would make an excellent weapon. Plants take a lot more energy to digest than meat, so *Massospondylus* has a wider pelvis and a larger set of guts in order to process them properly. The neck is longer to get at more food higher up in the trees. Dinosaurs were the first four-legged ground dwellers to be able to feed higher off the ground than sprawling animals. Being able to get at this new food source allowed prosauropods (such as *Massospondylus*), and then sauropods, to become the dominant plant-eaters for the next 50 million years.

For a long time, prosauropods were considered to be the ancestors of true sauropods because they look like smaller versions of the true sauropods. But there are some problems with this theory. Their foot anatomy is different enough from that of true sauropods to suggest that they are just a side branch that died out.

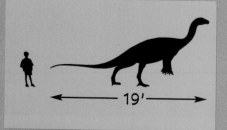

← 19' →

Comparison is with a 4-foot child

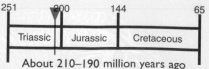

251	200	144	65
Triassic	Jurassic	Cretaceous	

About 210–190 million years ago

MEGALOSAURUS

MEG-a-lo-SAWR-us

(year named: 1824)

Megalosaurus ("giant lizard") was the first Mesozoic dinosaur to be named. For centuries, fragments of meat-eating dinosaurs had been found, but scientists thought these came from giant human beings (!) or elephants.

Then around 1815, Reverend William Buckland, a scientist at the University of Oxford, came across the remains of a jawbone with teeth, leg bones, and other parts of a skeleton. The teeth reminded Buckland of those of the monitor lizards, meat-eating lizards of the modern world. But these teeth and bones came from a reptile far larger than any monitor lizard!

In 1822, this new creature was given the name *Megalosaurus*. Buckland did not call his creature a dinosaur. That word would not be invented until 1842.

No complete *Megalosaurus* skeleton has yet been found. However, we can compare the bones we *have* found to more complete theropods and see that *Megalosaurus* was a two-legged predator with short but powerful arms. It seems to have been the largest meat-eater on land in Europe during the Middle Jurassic Period.

FUN FACTS: The book *Bleak House* by Charles Dickens (published in 1853) begins with the author imagining a 40-foot-long *Megalosaurus* "waddling like an elephantine lizard" up a muddy street in London.

LOCATION: England, possibly France

FOOD: Sauropods, stegosaurs

SIZE: About 25 feet (7.5 m) long, 6.1 feet (1.9 m) high at the hips

WEIGHT: 1.1 ton

TRIVIA: In the early days of paleontology, any meat-eating dinosaur fossils were considered to come from *Megalosaurus*; however, as more and better skeletons were found, scientists realized how diverse the meat-eating dinosaurs truly were.

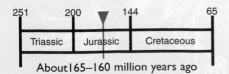

251	200		144	65
Triassic	Jurassic		Cretaceous	

About 165–160 million years ago

25'

Comparison is with a 4-foot child

METRIACANTHOSAURUS

met-ree-a-KAN-tho-SAWR-us

(year named: 1964)

FUN FACTS: Most dinosaurs are known from only one very incomplete fossil, like *Metriacan-thosaurus*.

LOCATION: England

FOOD: Sauropods, stegosaurs

SIZE: Perhaps 23 feet (7 m) long, almost 6 feet (1.8 m) high at the hips

WEIGHT: Maybe 1 ton

TRIVIA: *Metriacan-thosaurus* gets its name from its backbones, which have spines on top that are taller than in many meat-eaters (such as *Allosaurus* or *Tyrannosaurus*) but much smaller than those of *Spin-osaurus*.

Metriacanthosaurus ("moderate spine lizard") is one of the many dinosaurs that paleontologists would like to know more about. In 1923, the great German paleontologist Friedrich von Huene wrote a scientific paper describing all the theropod (or meat-eating) dinosaur fossils from the Jurassic and Cretaceous Periods of Europe. In his study, he examined a partial skeleton—an incomplete hip, a leg bone, and part of the backbone. He named it a new species of *Megalosaurus*. In 1964, however, scientist Alick Walker decided that these bones were too different from those of *Megalosaurus* and named the dinosaur *Metriacanthosaurus*.

Because so little is known about this dinosaur, any pictures of it or speculation on its habits are based on comparisons with meat-eating dinosaurs of which we have more complete skeletons. What is known is that this dinosaur was a theropod distinct from all the others. Perhaps someday more complete remains of this dinosaur will be found.

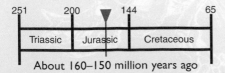

251 200 144 65

Triassic | Jurassic | Cretaceous

About 160–150 million years ago

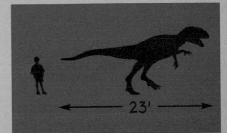

23'

Comparison is with a 4-foot child

MONOLOPHOSAURUS

MON-o-LOF-o-SAWR-us

(year named: 1993)

FUN FACTS: Many dinosaur fossils are found by accident. *Monolophosaurus*, for example, was found by geologists searching for oil deposits.

LOCATION: Xinjiang, China

FOOD: Sauropods, stegosaurs, early ankylosaurs

SIZE: Almost 17 feet (5.1 m) long, 5.6 feet (1.7 m) high at the hips

WEIGHT: 1,870 lbs (850 kg)

TRIVIA: *Monolophosaurus's* crest may have been brightly colored, but this is just a speculation. Unfortunately, color is not preserved in the fossil record.

Monolophosaurus ("single-crested lizard") was the top meat-eating dinosaur in China about the same time that *Megalosaurus* ruled England. In many ways it was a typical medium-sized Jurassic theropod: Its skull was about 2.25 feet (67 cm) long; i stood about 5.75 feet (1.7 m) high at the hips, and its jaws were filled with blade like teeth for slicing through meat.

The most outstanding feature o *Monolophosaurus* was its crest. Other meat-eating dinosaurs had crests or horns on their heads, but nothing quite like that of *Monolophosaurus*. The single fat crest ran from the tip of its nose to just above its eyes. The bones of this crest were hollow, but it was not connected to the windpipe, so it couldn't be used to make sounds the way that some duckbills could. Instead, this crest was probably hollow so that it didn't weigh down the dinosaur's head too much.

What could this crest have been for? Many modern animals have horns or fan tails or other features that are used for display, to show off in order to win mates or defend territory. It seems likely that *Monolophosaurus* did the same thing with its crest.

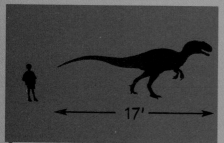

Comparison is with a 4-foot child

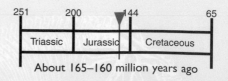

About 165–160 million years ago

MUTTABURRASAURUS

mutt-a-BUR-a-SAWR-us

(year named: 1981)

Muttaburrasaurus ("lizard from Muttaburra") has a stocky, well-muscled body. Although the only mounted skeleton in the world is shown with a thumb spike as big as *Iguanodon's*, some scientists question the restoration of this feature. That's because the original "spike" bone in *Muttaburrasaurus* is only partially preserved.

One feature *Muttaburrasaurus* has in common with later ornithopods, or two-legged plant-eating dinosaurs, is its large nose. It is not known if this nose allowed *Muttaburrasaurus* to communicate, as the hadrosaurs are believed to have done. The nose is closer to the tip of the snout than in hadrosaurs, but it is still large enough to block any stereoscopic vision directly ahead. Humans and predators have stereoscopic vision, which allows them to see in depth. Plant-eating dinosaurs and other prey have non-overlapping fields of vision, which gives them the ability to see more widely but hinders depth perception.

FUN FACTS: Because this dinosaur cannot be confidently placed within any known ornithopod family, it is considered a "free agent" (like an unsigned football player).

LOCATION: Australia

FOOD: Conifers, cycads, ginkgos

SIZE: 26 feet (8 m) long, about 10 feet (3 m) high at the hips

WEIGHT: 3 tons

FRIENDS: *Minmi*

ENEMIES: Theropods, or meat-eating dinosaurs

TRIVIA: The original specimen of *Muttaburrasaurus* was found in marine rocks. The dinosaur's body may have floated out to sea before fossilization.

251	200	144	65
Triassic	Jurassic	Cretaceous	

About 120–110 million years ago

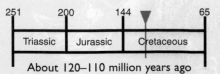

←——26'——→

Comparison is with a 4-foot child

NQWEBASAURUS

en-KWEB-ah-SAWR-us

(year named: 2000)

FUN FACTS: The first (and so far only) specimen of *Nqwebasaurus* was nicknamed "Kirky" for the Kirkwood Formation of rock in which it was found.

LOCATION: South Africa

FOOD: Possibly small mammals and reptiles, possibly insects

SIZE: 2.5 feet (80 cm) long, about 13 inches (33.3 cm) high at the hips

WEIGHT: 1.3 lbs (580 grams)

TRIVIA: "Kirky" was found with gizzard stones in its belly. Although it is well known that plant-eaters used "stomach stones" to help them grind up food, some meat-eating dinosaurs, such as the spinosaur *Baryonyx*, and crocodiles also used them.

Nqwebasaurus ("Nqweba lizard") is one of the smallest of all dinosaurs, except for birds. It is also one of the most recently discovered.

Two South African paleontologists, William De Klerk and Callum Ross, discovered the skeleton of this dinosaur in 1996. It was not complete, but the fossil clearly showed a small theropod (or meat-eating dinosaur), about 31 inches (80 cm) long. Like many theropods, it had a three-fingered hand. Its hind legs were long and built for running fast. When these paleontologists teamed up with American scientists to describe this dinosaur in 2000, they gave it the name *Nqwebasaurus* (Nqweba is the name of the Kirkwood region of South Africa—where this dinosaur was found—in the Xhosa language).

Nqwebasaurus is about the size of a chicken, as are *Compsognathus* and *Sinosauropteryx*. But unlike these other dinosaurs, its arms are relatively big. It probably could grab food with them. Because the teeth of *Nqwebasaurus* have not been found, we don't know if it ate mostly meat (such as small lizards or mammals), insects, or something else.

Comparison is with a 4-foot child

← 2.5' →

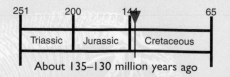

251	200	144	65
Triassic	Jurassic	Cretaceous	

About 135–130 million years ago

ORNITHOLESTES
or-NITH-o-LES-teez
(year named: 1903)

FUN FACTS: A famous painting by Charles R. Knight showed an *Ornitholestes* leaping after an *Archaeopteryx*. *Ornitholestes* may have eaten early birds, but *Archaeopteryx* itself lived in a different part of the world, and it is unlikely that even an agile hunter like *Ornitholestes* could have caught a bird in midair.

LOCATION: Wyoming

FOOD: Small mammals and reptiles, possibly including little dinosaurs

SIZE: 6.9 feet (2.1 m) long, 1.55 feet (0.47 m) high at the hips

WEIGHT: 27.7 lbs (12.6 kg)

TRIVIA: *Ornitholestes* is not the only small theropod from the Morrison Formation; another such dinosaur is called *Coelurus*.

Ornitholestes ("bird chief") is the best-known small theropod, or meat-eating dinosaur, from the famous Morrison Formation. The formation is a series of rocks in the western United States in which the best Late Jurassic dinosaur fossils in the world are found. The Morrison is well known for its sauropods (giant long-necked dinosaurs), impressive stegosaurs (plated dinosaurs), and giant meat-eaters such as *Allosaurus* and *Ceratosaurus*. However, small predators are also found in these rocks.

Ornitholestes is a small dinosaur, about 6.9 feet (2.1 m) long, half of which is tail. It has long arms—some paleontologists suggest that it could use these arms to catch birds. There is no evidence of this behavior, but primitive birds would have been about the proper size for this dinosaur to eat. More common victims may have been mammals, lizards, and baby dinosaurs.

The only known skull of *Ornitholestes* is damaged near the tip of its snout. It may have had a small horn over its nose.

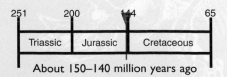

251	200	144	65
Triassic	Jurassic	Cretaceous	

About 150–140 million years ago

← 6.9' →

Comparison is with a 4-foot child

OTHNIELIA
OTH-NEE-lee-a

(year named: 1877)

FUN FACTS: The young of this small dinosaur would fit in your hand.

LOCATION: Colorado, Utah, Wyoming

FOOD: Ground plants and soft parts of conifers, cycads, ginkgos

SIZE: Less than 4 feet (1.1 m) long, about 1 foot (.3 m) high at the hips

WEIGHT: 50 pounds (22.7 kg)

FRIENDS: *Dryosaurus, Nanosaurus, Camptosaurus*

ENEMIES: Juvenile theropods

TRIVIA: There are no mounted specimens on exhibit anywhere in the world.

Othnielia (after Othniel C. Marsh) was originally found in the 1870s at Garden Park near Canyon City, Colorado. This is one of the most famous Jurassic quarries in the world and has given the world such dinosaurs as *Allosaurus, Ceratosaurus,* and *Stegosaurus.*

Despite years of searching, scientists have not found many ornithopods from the Late Jurassic Period. What we do know is that most of these were small, fast, agile plant-eaters with a single row of leaf-cutting teeth. The arms were proportionally small, making these dinosaurs back-heavy. This gave them better balance while running on their well-muscled hind limbs. *Othnielia*'s teeth have a short crown with a root that extends four times longer. The dinosaur must have eaten soft plants, because the whole tooth is too small to eat any of the hard plant parts. (This left hard fibrous plants to be eaten by the larger sauropods.) As one of the smallest dinosaurs, *Othnielia* made good eating for the juveniles of bigger theropods. *Othnielia* fossils have been found from hatchling to juvenile sizes. No adult skeletons have yet been found.

Comparison is with a 4-foot child

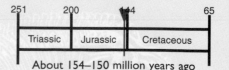

251	200	144	65
Triassic	Jurassic	Cretaceous	

About 154–150 million years ago

OVIRAPTOR
O-vi-RAP-tor

(year named: 1924

Oviraptor ("egg hunter") is a dinosaur once thought to have been an egg hunter. It is now known to have been an egg protector!

When paleontologists first found this little meat-eater in the Mongolian desert, it was sitting on top of a bunch of fossilized eggs. The scientists thought these eggs were from the horned dinosaur *Protoceratops*. Knowing that *Oviraptor* was a theropod, or meat-eating dinosaur, the scientists guessed that *Oviraptor* was about to *eat* the eggs. Many decades later, however, paleontologists discovered that these eggs were actually *Oviraptor* eggs, and that (like birds) *Oviraptors* sat on their eggs before they hatched. Since then, many *Oviraptor* nests (and nests of related dinosaurs) have been found with parents on top.

Oviraptor is one of the oviraptorosaur dinosaurs. Like other Late Cretaceous oviraptorosaurs, *Oviraptor* had a deep, toothless beak. It also had long, grasping hands, which would have been useful for clutching food.

The exact diet of *Oviraptor* is debated by paleontologists. The first skeleton of *Oviraptor* contained a lizard skeleton in its belly, so it definitely ate some meat. Some paleontologists, however, think that it may have eaten plants.

FUN FACTS: *Oviraptor*'s skull was so unusual that, when it was first being dug out of the rock, paleontologists were not sure which end was the front!

LOCATION: Mongolia, China

FOOD: Small reptiles (including baby dinosaurs), possibly also plants and eggs

SIZE: 7.6 feet (2.3 m) long, almost 2.5 feet (0.75 m) high at the hips

WEIGHT: 71 lbs (32.4 kg)

TRIVIA: *Oviraptor* was originally going to be named *Fenestrosaurus* ("window lizard") because of the openings in its skull, but the paleontologist who named it thought that "egg hunter" was a more interesting name.

Comparison is with a 4-foot child

← 7.6' →

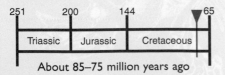

251	200	144	▼ 65
Triassic	Jurassic	Cretaceous	

About 85–75 million years ago

PACHYCEPHALOSAURUS

PAK-ee-SEF-a-lo-SAWR-us

(year named: 1931)

FUN FACTS: Males had larger and more ornamented bumps on the back of their skulls than females.

LOCATION: South Dakota, Wyoming

FOOD: Low-growing conifers, cycads, ginkgos, flowering plants

SIZE: Over 13 feet (about 4 m) long, over 5 feet (1.6 m) high at the hips

WEIGHT: 800 pounds (364 kg)

FRIENDS: Hadrosaurs, small ceratopsians (horned dinosaurs)

ENEMIES: *Troodon*, tyrannosaurs, dromaeosaurs

← 12' →

Comparison is with a 4-foot child

Pachycephalosaurus ("thick-headed lizard") is the last and mos famous member of the Pachycephalosauria, or thick-headed dinosaurs. In the 1970s, paleontologist Peter Galton proposed that male pachycephalosaurs used their domed heads as battering rams, like bighorn sheep. The idea caught the public's imagination. In *The Lost World: Jurassic Park*, you can even see the dome-headed pachycephalosaurs doing hea butts (of course, these are geneticall engineered dinosaurs and not necessar ily the exact same ones that lived 7 million years ago!). But by the 1990s, sci entists began to question Galton's head butting theory. It was pointed out tha animals who do butt heads have a wide surface area where the heads come into contact to prevent "head slippage." Thi happens when two animals butt heads a high speed and do not hit straight on They risk breaking their necks when their heads suddenly snap to one side *Pachycephalosaurus* has a domed, o rounded, head, which would minimize surface contact and therefore increase the risk of head slippage.

TRIVIA: The teeth of *Pachycephalosaurus* are smaller than the first teeth of a human baby!

TAKE TWO!
In the second *Jurassic Park* movie, two genetically engineered *Pachycephalosaurus* were shown butting heads like billy goats. But the actual *Pachycephalosaurus* did not have the proper build for such impact. It is more likely they used their heads as weapons against meat-eating enemies!

This throws doubt on the idea of any high-speed head-butting between pachycephalosaurs, but it does not exclude "head-pushing" or "head-ramming" against non-pachycephalosaurs. It just happens that if a pachycephalosaur lowered its head and charged at a theropod, the impact would be right at the level of the theropod's head or pelvis—the perfect place to stop an attacker. Since *Pachycephalosaurus* had a skull up to 9 inches (23 cm) thick, guess who'd lose?

251	200	144	65
Triassic	Jurassic	Cretaceous	

About 70–65 million years ago

PARASAUROLOPHUS and CHARONOSAURUS

PAR-a-saw-ROL-o-fus   ka-RO-no-SAWR-us

(year named: 1922)   (year named: 2000)

Charonosaurus

FUN FACTS: If you want to hear what *Parasaurolophus* sounds like, go to *www.nmmnh-abq.mus.nm.us/ nmmnh/soundandimages.html*

LOCATION: *Charonosaurus* in China, *Parasaurolophus* in New Mexico; Utah; Montana; Alberta, Canada

FOOD: Conifers, cycads, ginkgos, flowering plants

SIZE: 40 feet (over 12 m) long, about 9 feet (2.8 m) high at the hips

WEIGHT: 2 tons

FRIENDS: *Edmontosaurus*

ENEMIES: *Tyrannosaurus, Tarbosaurus*

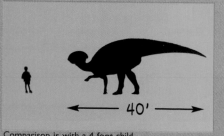

← 40' →

Comparison is with a 4-foot child

Parasaurolophus ("like *Saurolophus*") and *Charonosaurus* ("Charon's lizard") are two very closely related duckbill dinosaurs. They have one major feature in common: a long nasal tube. This hollow tube has up to three paired chambers that connect the nostrils with the back of the throat. Scientists Thomas Williamson and Robert Sullivan have studied these chambers with a computer axial tomography (CAT) scan. They theorize that these dinosaurs could not only make sounds within the range of human hearing but also in "infra-sound," or below the range of human hearing, like modern elephants!

The nasal tube also served other purposes and is the perfect example of a multi-function device. It aided species recognition during mating, enhanced the dinosaur's sense of smell, humidified the air it breathed, and indicated how old it was.

Charonosaurus is from China and *Parasaurolophus* is from western North America. This indicates that these areas

Parasaurolophus

were connected by a land bridge at the end of the Cretaceous Period. They are both lambeosaurs, or crested duckbills. Lambeosaurs made up a larger percentage of the herbivore communities in Asia than in North America, where flat-headed hadrosaurs and horned dinosaurs are more common. This means that although the two areas were connected, they had different fauna.

TAKE TWO!
In _The Lost World: Jurassic Park_, a safari team set out to capture a number of dinosaurs. This shot of a _Parasaurolophus_ running from one of the caravan vehicles is the best restoration of a _Parasaurolophus_ yet rendered in a movie.

TRIVIA: The _Parasaurolophus_ specimen on display at the Royal Ontario Museum in Toronto has two broken back bones.

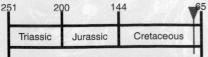

251	200	144	65
Triassic	Jurassic	Cretaceous	

About 75–65 million years ago

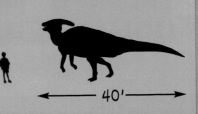

← 40' →

Comparison is with a 4-foot child

PELECANIMIMUS
pel-e-KAN-i-MIME-us
(year named: 1994)

FUN FACTS: *Pelecanimimus* was preserved in mud at the bottom of an ancient lagoon. The same rock contains the remains of many plants, insects, fish, lizards, crocodiles, and at least three bird species.

LOCATION: Spain

FOOD: Possibly fish, possibly small reptiles and mammals

SIZE: 6.6 feet (2 m) long, about 20 inches (50 cm) high at the hips

WEIGHT: About 26 lbs (12 kg)

FRIENDS: None

ENEMIES: Larger theropods

TRIVIA: *Pelecanimimus* has more teeth than any other dinosaur known.

*P*elecanimimus ("pelican mimic") is the earliest known ornithomosaur, or "bird mimic," often called an ostrich dinosaur. It lived during the early part of the Cretaceous Period, whereas most ostrich dinosaurs lived millions of years later, during the Late Cretaceous Period.

Like other ornithomimosaurs, *Pelecanimimus* has a small, pointed head at the end of a long neck. Its arms end in typical ostrich dinosaur hands—three fingers of the same length, all curving in the same direction. But unlike the Late Cretaceous ostrich dinosaurs, which have toothless beaks, *Pelecanimimus* has jaws filled with over 220 tiny teeth. It is also the smallest known ostrich dinosaur, being only 6.6 feet (2 m) long.

Pelecanimimus is known only from a single skeleton from Spain. On that skeleton, an impression of skin was found around some of the bones. The impression indicated that there was a pouch underneath the lower jaw, like that of a pelican. However, when scientists examined these impressions more closely, they realized that these were not the outside surface of the skin but the inside tissue! This was one of the first times that a dinosaur's muscle tissue had been preserved. Unfortunately, because the fossilization process turned this tissue into rock, none of its DNA was preserved.

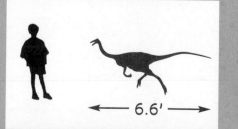

← 6.6' →

Comparison is with a 4-foot child

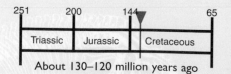

251	200	144		65
Triassic	Jurassic		Cretaceous	

About 130–120 million years ago

PLATEOSAURUS
PLAT-ee-o-SAWR-us

(year named: 1837)

Plateosaurus ("flat lizard") is an early dinosaur from the Triassic Period. It was the first dinosaur that was much larger than a human, and the first with a long sauropod-like neck. *Plateosaurus* was heavily built, and its long muzzle was filled with teeth designed for chopping. The feet were clawed, and the hands had some grasping ability. The hand claw was relatively small compared to that of *Massospondylus* (see page 92). Many outdated skeletons show *Plateosaurus* walking on two feet. But that is unlikely because *Plateosaurus* was big and front-heavy and likely walked on all four feet.

Plateosaurus has been studied many times, mainly by the German paleontologist Friedrich von Huene in the early 1900s and by Peter Galton in the late 1900s. Galton challenged the theory that *Plateosaurus* was an omnivore, or plant- *and* meat-eater. He showed that its teeth and jaw action were more like that of a true plant-eater, where the lower jaws meet the upper jaws like a nutcracker, with all the teeth coming together at the same time. In an omnivore, the jaws come together more like scissors, with the teeth meeting first at the back of the jaw, then finally at the front of the jaw.

FUN FACTS: Over a hundred *Plateosaurus* skeletons have been found.
LOCATION: Germany, France, Switzerland
FOOD: Conifers, cycads, ginkgos
SIZE: 26 feet (8 m) long, over 6.6 feet (2 m) high at the hips
WEIGHT: 1 ton
FRIENDS: *Sellosaurus*
ENEMIES: *Liliensternus*
TRIVIA: *Plateosaurus* was named in 1837, *before* the word "dinosaur" was coined!

251	200	144	65
Triassic	Jurassic	Cretaceous	

About 220–210 million years ago

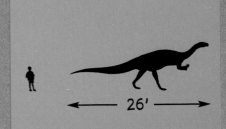

26'

Comparison is with a 4-foot child

107

PROCOMPSOGNATHUS
pro-komp-SOG-na-thus
(year named: 1914)

FUN FACTS: *Procompsognathus* was so small that a small dog or a house cat would have been a danger to it. Good thing for *Procompsognathus* that dogs and cats did not evolve until 200 million years after it was gone!

LOCATION: Germany

FOOD: Possibly small mammals, reptiles, and insects

SIZE: Less than 3 feet (90 cm) long, 10 inches (26 cm) high at the hips

WEIGHT: 2.2 lbs (1 kg)

FRIENDS: None

ENEMIES: Crocodile relatives

TRIVIA: *Procompsognathus* is one of the smallest dinosaurs known from the Triassic Period.

Comparison is with a 4-foot child

Procompsognathus ("before *Compsognathus*") is a very small dinosaur from the Late Triassic Period. The only known skeleton of this dinosaur is incomplete but shows that it was less than 3 feet (90 cm) long. It is a small theropod, or meat-eating dinosaur, and ran on long hind legs.

The paleontologists who first discovered this fossil thought it reminded them of *Compsognathus*, the little theropod from the Late Jurassic of Germany. More recent studies of this dinosaur show that it was more closely related to *Coelophysis* and *Dilophosaurus* than to *Compsognathus*. Also, these studies show that the skull that was originally thought to be from *Procompsognathus* was actually from an early land-living crocodile relative.

There is no evidence that *Procompsognathus* (or *Compsognathus*) ran around in packs, attacking much larger animals.

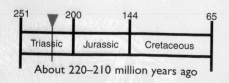

251		200	144	65
	Triassic	Jurassic	Cretaceous	

About 220–210 million years ago

PROSAUROLOPHUS
PRO-sawr-o-LO-fus

(year named: 1916)

Prosaurolophus ("before *Saurolophus*") is a duckbill dinosaur, one of the two-legged herbivorous dinosaurs known as ornithopods. It is a relatively unknown dinosaur, in need of a publicist. The first specimen was collected by the greatest dinosaur field paleontologist of the twentieth century, Barnum Brown of the American Museum of Natural History in New York. During World War I, Brown led an expedition along the Red Deer River in Alberta, Canada, where he collected some of the most perfect duckbill skeletons ever found—including this one.

Prosaurolophus (and its probable descendant, *Saurolophus*) belongs to a subgroup of duckbills known as the Saurolophini, the rarest of all duckbills. These dinosaurs are sometimes hard to place in the "big picture" of duckbill evolution because they have features from both the hadrosaurines, or non-crested duckbills, and the lambeosaurines, or crested duckbills.

FUN FACTS: There are two species of *Prosaurolophus*. One was named by Jack Horner, the duckbill expert who inspired the character of Alan Grant in the *Jurassic Park* movies.

LOCATION: Montana; Alberta, Canada

FOOD: Conifers, cycads, ginkgos, flowering plants

SIZE: About 33 feet (10 m) long, 6 feet (1.8 m) high at the hips

WEIGHT: 2 tons

TRIVIA: There are fewer duckbill experts than there are specimens of *Prosaurolophus*!

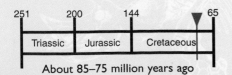

251	200	144	65
Triassic	Jurassic	Cretaceous	

About 85–75 million years ago

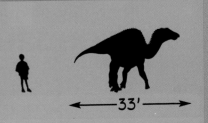

33'

Comparison is with a 4-foot child

PSITTACOSAURUS
sih-TAK-o-SAWR-us
(year named: 1931)

Raptor foot

FUN FACTS: Ceratopsians are so popular that they have their own book, *The Horned Dinosaurs,* by Peter Dodson.
LOCATION: China, Mongolia, Thailand
FOOD: Conifers, cycads, ginkgos
SIZE: 6.6 feet (2 m) long, almost 20 inches (.5 m) high at the hips
WEIGHT: 50 pounds (23 kg)
FRIENDS: *Shamosaurus, Altirhinus*
ENEMIES: *Harpymimus, Chilantaisaurus*
TRIVIA: *Psittacosaurus* has horns on its cheeks, called jugal horns.

← 6.6' →

Comparison is with a 4-foot child

Psittacosaurus ("parrot lizard") was one of the first to appear of the last great group of dinosaurs: ceratopsia, the horned dinosaurs. *Psittacosaurus* has two features common to all ceratopsians: an extra upper beak bone on top of the upper lip bone, and the beginnings of what will become the ceratopsian frill.

Over eleven species of *Psittacosaurus* have been named—more than in 99 percent of all other dinosaurs. But are they all valid? Some scientists will name a new species based on very slight differences in the skull. These differences can be the result, however, of sex, age, health, and normal variation within populations. There are also stratigraphic differences. This means that over time, later populations can evolve larger features than their ancestors.

Psittacosaurus remains have been found with gastroliths, or stomach stones. Because most herbivorous dinosaurs could not chew their food, they swallowed a lot of unprocessed plants. To aid their digestion, they also swallowed small stones.

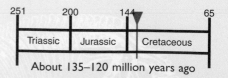

251	200	144		65
Triassic	Jurassic		Cretaceous	

About 135–120 million years ago

SAUROPOSEIDON

SAWR-o-po-SIE-don

(year named: 2000)

S auroposeidon ("Poseidon lizard," after the Greek god of earthquakes) is the tallest dinosaur yet known to science. It was found in 1994 but not named until 2000. That is because it takes several years to prepare and analyze such a large skeleton. The bones of this sauropod, or long-necked plant-eater, are so big, when they were first discovered, some scientists thought they'd found a fossilized tree trunk!

Sauroposeidon's neck is about 40 feet (12 m) long! A single neck bone is over 5 feet (1.6 m)! These neck bones are so hollow that when X-rayed, they show more space than bone. This is a biological phenomenon called "structural lightening." It is designed to allow large bones to support great weights without weighing too much themselves. An adult human standing next to Sauroposeidon would not even come up to its elbow!

FUN FACTS: Sauroposeidon was the last member of the family Brachiosauridae before they went extinct. This is the tallest known animal (so far) in Earth's history.

LOCATION: Oklahoma

FOOD: Conifers, cycads, ginkgos

SIZE: About 100 feet (over 31m) long, 13 feet (4m) high at the hips

WEIGHT: 50 tons

TRIVIA: The largest living mammals are still not as well engineered as the dinosaurs. Mammal bones are more solid and less able to handle larger weight loads.

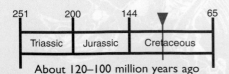

251	200	144	65
Triassic	Jurassic	Cretaceous	

About 120–100 million years ago

60'

Comparison is with a 4-foot child

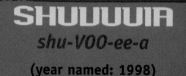

SHUVUUIA
shu-VOO-ee-a
(year named: 1998)

Shuvuuia ("bird") is one of the strangest theropods, or meat-eating dinosaurs, ever found. It is one of the alvarezsaurs, a group of small bird-like dinosaurs of the Late Cretaceous Period.

Shuvuuia has a pointed, beaky snout, with jaws holding many very tiny teeth. It has a long neck, a compact body, a fairly short tail (for a dinosaur), and long legs built for running fast.

One of the oddest parts about it is its arms. While most advanced theropods had three working fingers, and the tyrant dinosaurs had two, alvarezsaurs had only one working finger—the thumb. Also, although the arms of Shuvuuia are short—like its larger relatives—they were extremely strong. Scientists do not know how Shuvuuia used these arms, but they certainly had some function. Perhaps it used them to dig into insect nests?

Shuvuuia and the other alvarezsaurs are a bit of a puzzle in the dinosaur family tree. In some ways they seem like the ostrich dinosaurs, in others they are similar to primitive birds, and in still other ways they are like troodonts. Paleontologists are still trying to determine the closest relatives to these bizarre little dinosaurs.

FUN FACTS: A skeleton of Shuvuuia is on display at the American Museum of Natural History in New York City.
LOCATION: Mongolia
FOOD: Possibly insects, possibly small mammals and reptiles
SIZE: About 3 feet (.88 m) long, 12 inches (30 cm) high at the hips
WEIGHT: About 5.5 lbs (2.5 kg)
FRIENDS: None
ENEMIES: Velociraptor
TRIVIA: A full-grown Shuvuuia was only the size of a chicken, but it was bigger than most of the mammals that lived in its environment.

Comparison is with a 4-foot child

← 3' →

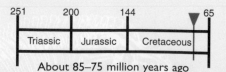

251	200	144	65
Triassic	Jurassic	Cretaceous	

About 85–75 million years ago

SINORNITHOIDES
sie-NOR-ni-THOI-deez

(year named: 1993)

Sinornithoides ("Chinese bird form") is one of the oldest known troodonts, or "wounding tooth" dinosaurs. Troodonts were meat-eating dinosaurs with extremely long hind legs. They were very bird-like in the details of their braincases, their backbones, and other features. They were also probably among the fastest of the smaller dinosaurs.

Before *Sinornithoides* was discovered, troodonts were only known from incomplete fossils. Then, in 1988, the skeleton of this little dinosaur was found in the region of China called Inner Mongolia. This dinosaur had been buried by a sandstorm while lying on its belly. Its head and neck were tucked under its arm, and its tail was wrapped around its body. Because it was covered over so quickly and so completely, nearly the entire skeleton was preserved in fine detail.

Sinornithoides was about the size of a wild turkey. It could easily chase down mammals, lizards, smaller dinosaurs (including babies), and similar creatures for their meat. Because the teeth of troodonts are similar to those of plant-eating dinosaurs, some scientists think that troodonts like *Sinornithoides* also ate insects and plants. Many small carnivorous mammals (foxes and raccoons, for instance) are actually omnivores: They eat meat, plants, and other food.

FUN FACTS: *Sinornithoides* is not the only Asian troodont. There are several other kinds, including one called *Borogovia* after the borogoves in Lewis Carroll's poem "Jabberwocky."

LOCATION: Inner Mongolia, China

FOOD: Mammals, lizards, smaller dinosaurs, possibly insects, possibly plants

SIZE: About 3.6 feet (1.1 m) long, almost 18 inches (45 cm) high at the hips

WEIGHT: About 12 lbs (5.5 kg)

FRIENDS: None

ENEMIES: Larger theropods

TRIVIA: Until *Sinornithoides* was found, many paleontologists thought that troodonts had long arms like raptors.

251	200	144	65
Triassic	Jurassic	Cretaceous	

About 110–100 million years ago

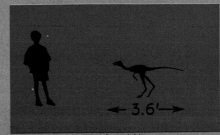

← 3.6' →

Comparison is with a 4-foot child

113

SINORNITHOSAURUS
SIEN-or-nith-o-SAWR-us

(year named: 1999)

FUN FACTS: A raptor from Montana that was very similar in size to *Sinornithosaurus* was named *Bambiraptor* because its long legs reminded the discoverers of the fictional deer Bambi.

LOCATION: Liaoning Province, China

FOOD: *Psittacosaurus, Sinosauropteryx, Caudipteryx, Beipiaosaurus, Confuciusornis*

Sinornithosaurus ("Chinese bird lizard") is one of the oldest known dromaeosaurs, or raptors. This was an early relative of *Velociraptor* and *Deinonychus*. Like *Velociraptor*, it was a fairly small dinosaur, but it was probably very dangerous. It had sharp, curved teeth in its jaws, long grasping hands at the end of long arms, and a killer sickle claw on the second toe of each foot. What makes *Sinornithosaurus* more famous, though, is that fact that it was "fuzzy"!

All over the body of *Sinornithosaurus* were long filaments. These structures were protofeathers, a fuzzy body covering that eventually evolved into true feathers. Both protofeathers and true feathers are "soft" features that do not fossilize easily. But the fine-grained mud of the Yixian Formation, where *Sinornithosaurus* was found, was able to preserve the soft features of the dinosaurs, other animals, and plants that died there.

Other theropods found in the Yixian Formation include *Beipiaosaurus, Caudipteryx, Confuciusornis,* and *Sinosauropteryx.* They all were found to have

Comparison is with a 4-foot child

either protofeathers or true feathers. Before these finds, scientists thought that raptor dinosaurs like *Deinonychus* and *Velociraptor* were covered only in scales. This is because the rocks where they were found did not preserve their soft body coverings.

Now, with the discovery of *Sinornithosaurus* (and the other theropods found in the Yixian), we know that raptors and all the other advanced, bird-like meat-eating dinosaurs were covered with either fuzzy protofeathers or true feathers.

SIZE: About 4 feet (1.25 m) long, about 18 inches (over 45 cm) high at the hips

WEIGHT: 12 pounds (6.4 kg)

FRIENDS: None

ENEMIES: None

TRIVIA: The first detailed study of the body covering of *Sinornithosaurus* was published in March 2001. It showed that much of this little dinosaur was covered by down, like the fluff on the body of baby chicks. Some of this dinosaur's protofeathers, however, were longer shafts with branches coming off of them, like the feathers of modern adult birds.

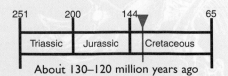

251   200   144   65

| Triassic | Jurassic | Cretaceous |

About 130–120 million years ago

SINOSAUROPTERYX

SIEN-o-sawr-ROP-te-riks

(year named: 1996)

FUN FACTS: Although its name means "Chinese lizard wing," *Sinosauropteryx* did not have wings, nor could it fly. In fact, its arms were so short that they could barely scratch its knee!

LOCATION: Liaoning Province, China

FOOD: Small mammals and lizards

SIZE: A little over 4 feet (1.25 m) long, 11.4 inches (29 cm) high at the hips

WEIGHT: 5.5 lbs (2.5 kg)

FRIENDS: *Psittacosaurus, Caudipteryx, Beipiaosaurus, Confuciusornis*

ENEMIES: *Sinornithosaurus*

TRIVIA: The scientists who discovered *Sinosauropteryx* at first thought that dinosaurs could not have feathers, so they called it a bird.

Comparison is with a 4-foot child

*S*inosauropteryx ("Chinese lizard wing") was probably the most important dinosaur discovered in the 1990s. Before it was found, paleontologists had shown that birds were the descendants of theropods, meat-eating dinosaurs. However, they did not know *when* certain bird-like features first appeared. That's because many of the things that make birds special among all living animals are soft features that don't fossilize well.

One of these soft features is feathers. Some paleontologists suspected that many of the theropod dinosaurs were actually covered by feathers or fuzz, but they could not find proof. Then, in 1996, an amazing discovery was made in northeastern China. In a series of rocks called the Yixian Formation, the skeleton of a small theropod was found. This little dinosaur was very similar to *Compsognathus,* a slightly older dinosaur from Germany. The bones of the skeleton were complete, but the most interesting thing about the fossil was the traces of small fibers surrounding the bones. These fibers turned out to be protofeathers, a simple type of body covering that developed into feathers in birds and their closest relatives.

Since 1996, many feathered dinosaurs have been found in the Yixian Formation, but *Sinosauropteryx* is the most primitive of the feathered dinosaurs found to date. Because the

Yixian dig has revealed that *Sinosauropteryx,* as well as its more advanced relatives, had feathers or protofeathers, paleontologists now realize that almost all the advanced meat-eating dinosaurs had this covering. This includes not only little dinosaurs like troodonts (see *Sinornithoides*) and alvarezsaurs (see *Shuvuuia*), but also medium-sized forms like ostrich dinosaurs (see *Pelecanimimus* and *Gallimimus*), oviraptorosaurs (see *Oviraptor* and *Caudipteryx*), and dromaeosaur raptors (see *Sinornithosaurus, Velociraptor,* and *Deinonychus*). Even *Tyrannosaurus, Gorgosaurus,* and the other tyrant dinosaurs (which are more advanced than *Sinosauropteryx*) probably had protofeathers when they were hatchlings, but some scientists think that they might have shed these as they grew up.

You might wonder why the Yixian Formation was able to preserve the soft features of these dinosaurs, while other rocks did not. The mud that became the Yixian Formation is very fine-grained— that is, the particles that make it up are very small. Because of this, small details were not blurred out. Also, because these dinosaurs were preserved in a quiet lake-like environment, rather than in muds dumped by a flooding river or sands blown around by sandstorms, the bodies of the dinosaurs were not damaged before they were covered over with mud. Thanks to this lucky circumstance, we now know much more about the outsides of these dinosaurs!

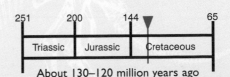

251	200	144	65
Triassic	Jurassic	Cretaceous	

About 130–120 million years ago

SPINOSAURUS
SPIEN-o-SAWR-us
(year named: 1915)

FUN FACTS: Old pictures of *Spinosaurus* showed it incorrectly with a *Tyrannosaurus*-like skull.
LOCATION: Egypt, Morocco
FOOD: Other dinosaurs, large fish
SIZE: Perhaps over 46 feet (14 m) long, 18.5 feet (5.6 m) high (including sail)
WEIGHT: Perhaps 8 tons
TRIVIA: *Spinosaurus* is not the only dinosaur with a sail. *Ouranosaurus* (a relative of *Iguanodon*) also had a sail. The sail-backed *Dimetrodon* of the Permian Period was *not* a dinosaur. It was, in fact, a primitive

*S*pinosaurus ("spine lizard") is one of the most spectacular dinosaurs ever found. It was an enormous meat-eating dinosaur, as big as *Tyrannosaurus rex*. But its jaws and teeth were very different from *T. rex*'s. The jaws were long and slender, and the teeth were cone-shaped, like those of a crocodile.

Its most distinctive feature, however, was the huge sail-like fin on its back. This sail was made from the spines that come out of the top of the backbones of dinosaurs and all other backboned animals. If you feel down your spine from the bottom of your head, you'll feel a series of bumps (especially at the base of the neck). These bumps are the same bumps on the top of backbones of dinosaurs. The spines of *Spinosaurus*, though, were tremendous: The longest one found was over 5 feet (1.7 m) tall!

What would have been the purpose of such a sail? Although *Spinosaurus* lived in a swampy coastal environment, the sail would not have been used like

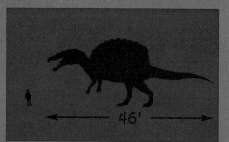

46'

Comparison is with a 4-foot child

synapsid (or protomammal), more closely related to the ancestors of mammals.

the sail of a boat. Instead, it may have served to let *Spinosaurus* cool itself down if it got too hot. The skin on the sail, like all skin, would have been filled with blood vessels. Hot blood pumped into the sail would be cooled off, especially if there was a breeze; African elephants use blood vessels in their ears for this purpose. Also, the sail might have been used to show off to other *Spinosaurus*, either to attract a mate or to defend its territory.

Additionally, the dinosaur may have used its sail to make itself look bigger. Living in the same environment as *Spinosaurus* were a couple of other giant predators, *Carcharodontosaurus* and *Deltadromeus*. If a *Spinosaurus* turned itself sideways toward an attacker, it would suddenly look much larger, and so the other predator might think twice about attacking. Modern cats do something similar: When they get scared, they puff up their fur to make themselves look larger.

TAKE TWO!

A *Spinosaurus* is one of the dinosaur stars of the third *Jurassic Park* movie. In it, *Spinosaurus* fights *Tyrannosaurus*. Which was stronger? Paleontologists will never know for certain. In fact, *Spinosaurus* and *Tyrannosaurus* never met: They lived on different continents and were separated by tens of millions of years. So *Spinosaurus* and *T. rex* could fight only in movies (or in our imagination).

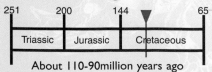

251	200	144	65
Triassic	Jurassic	Cretaceous	

About 110-90 million years ago

STEGOSAURUS

STEG-o-SAWR-us
(year named: 1877)

FUN FACTS: Almost everything in popular books about *Stegosaurus* is based on the specimen at the Smithsonian in Washington, D.C.
LOCATION: Colorado, Wyoming, Utah
FOOD: Plants
SIZE: About 25 feet (7.5 m) long, 7 feet (2.1 m) high at the hips
WEIGHT: 3 tons
TRIVIA: *Stegosaurus* comes in two varieties: a large-plated species with four long tail spikes and a rarer, smaller-plated species with shorter tail spikes (possibly eight of them), based on a partial specimen. The second species may not be valid.

*S*tegosaurus ("roofed lizard") is the best-known "plated" dinosaur. It was a favorite food of *Allosaurus* and has been well studied by paleontologists for over 125 years. It has also been the subject of many false "dinosaur myths"—among them that it had a brain no bigger than a walnut (it was, in fact, more than twice as big as a walnut), a second brain in its hips, and plates that could flap on command.

Several questions about *Stegosaurus* have received a lot of study by scientists in the 1990s. It has been proposed at various times that *Stegosaurus* had either one or two rows of plates along its back. A new specimen found by Ken Carpenter, Bryan Small, and a team at the Denver Museum of Natural History shows that *Stegosaurus* did have a double row of alternating plates down its back. This new specimen also shows that the tail spikes did not point upward—as in most museum exhibits—but instead pointed sideways.

← 25' →

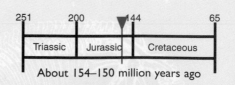

251	200	▼144	65
Triassic	Jurassic	Cretaceous	

About 154–150 million years ago

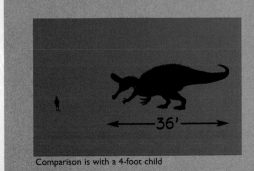

SUCHOMIMUS
SOOK-o-MIEM-us
(year named: 1998)

Suchomimus ("crocodile mimic") is a spinosaur dinosaur, related to *Baryonyx* and *Spinosaurus*. Like them, it had a long, narrow snout packed with crocodile-like teeth and a huge thumb claw. Although it was larger than *Baryonyx*, it was smaller than the gigantic *Spinosaurus*.

Suchomimus was given the name "crocodile mimic" because, like a crocodile, its skull was long and slender and its teeth were shaped like cones (unlike many of the meat-eaters, which had blade-like teeth). Some paleontologists think that this means they ate mostly fish. It is true that *Suchomimus* lived near water, and that the remains of 10-foot (3-m) fish were found with it in the same rocks. This suggests that *Suchomimus* waded into the water and grabbed fish with its jaws, or hooked them with its thumb claw.

Today's big crocodilians eat both large fish and land animals. *Suchomimus*, too, could have hunted the big land animals of its day—other dinosaurs. Its jaws could kill a dinosaur as easily as they could a fish.

FUN FACTS: Another dinosaur from the same rock formation as *Suchomimus* is the sail-backed *Ouranosaurus*, a relative of *Iguanodon*.

LOCATION: Niger, northern Africa

FOOD: Large fish, dinosaurs

SIZE: 36 feet (11 m) long, 12 feet (3.6 m) high at the hips

WEIGHT: 5 tons

FRIENDS: None

ENEMIES: None

TRIVIA: The thumb claw was one of the first bones found for both *Baryonyx* and *Suchomimus*.

251	200	144	65
Triassic	Jurassic	Cretaceous	

About 110–100 million years ago

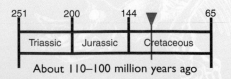

36'

Comparison is with a 4-foot child

THERIZINOSAURUS
THER-ih-ZEE-no-SAWR-us
(year named: 1954)

FUN FACTS:
Therizinosaurus has the largest finger bones of any known animal in Earth's history.
LOCATION: Mongolia
FOOD: Conifers, ginkgos, possibly flowering plants
SIZE: About 23 feet (7 m) long, over 10 feet (3 m) high at the hips
WEIGHT: 3 tons
FRIENDS: *Saurolophus*
ENEMIES: *Tarbosaurus* (a relative of *Tyrannosaurus*)
TRIVIA: When paleontologists first found *Therizinosaurus,* they thought it was some kind of giant turtle!

Therizinosaurus ("scythe lizard") is enormous. It i also one of the most bizarr dinosaurs. Although it is a thero pod (or meat-eating) dinosaur, i most likely ate just plants! It ha gigantic claws, the largest over 2 inches (70 cm) long. But thes claws were not curved an hooked like the claws of predator. Instead, they wer flat and straight.

Therizinosaurus was a giant rel ative of *Beipiaosaurus*. That earlie dinosaur was covered by protofeathers a simple body covering that in som other dinosaurs (including ovirap torosaurs and birds) became true feath ers. Because the earlier therizinosau *Beipiaosaurus* had these protofeathers paleontologists suspect that *Ther izinosaurus* had them, too.

Therizinosaurus's upper arm bone i almost 3 feet (.88 m) long. It may have been used to break branches off o trees.

It may seem strange to think of plant-eater as a member of a group o meat-eating animals, but this is not the only case of that happening. For exam ple, the modern giant panda eats almos nothing except bamboo, but it is a mem ber of the carnivorous mammal group.

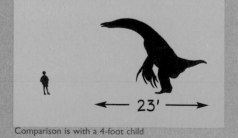

← 23' →

Comparison is with a 4-foot child

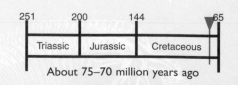

251	200	144	65
Triassic	Jurassic	Cretaceous	

About 75–70 million years ago

THESCELOSAURUS
THES-sel-o-SAWR-us

(year named: 1913)

Thescelosaurus ("marvelous lizard") was originally collected in Wyoming in 1891 by legendary field paleontologist John Bell Hatcher. He shipped it back to his employer, Professor Othniel C. Marsh, at Yale University. It stayed packed up and ignored until the turn of the century. It was then given to the Smithsonian Institution as a part of the Marsh Collection. And there it remained, *still* packed up, until 1913. When Charles Gilmore finally unpacked it, he immediately knew the specimen was a new dinosaur. He named it *Thescelosaurus neglectus,* or "marvelous but neglected lizard"!

Thescelosaurus is part of the ornithopod family Hypsilophodontidae. All its members have relatively small arms, well-muscled legs, and a stiffened tail. Most known specimens are from juveniles.

One rare adult *Thescelosaurus* specimen made worldwide headlines in 2000. It was sold by a commercial collector and nicknamed "Willo." It has a nodule inside the chest cavity that a few scientists believe is a fossilized heart. The specimen is now under intense study.

FUN FACTS: Skin samples (which are very rare!) are also known for this dinosaur.

LOCATION: Wyoming; South Dakota; Alberta and Saskatchewan, Canada

FOOD: Ground cover, such as cycads and flowering plants

SIZE: About 10 feet (over 3 m) long, about 3.5 feet (over 1 m) high at the hips

WEIGHT: 150 pounds (68 kg)

FRIENDS: *Edmontosaurus, Pachycephalosaurus, Triceratops*

ENEMIES: *Ornithomimus, Troodon, Dromaeosaurus*

TRIVIA: The original specimen is on display at the Smithsonian Institution in Washington, D.C.

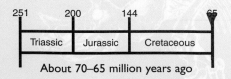

251	200	144	65
Triassic	Jurassic	Cretaceous	

About 70–65 million years ago

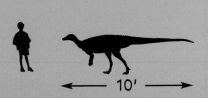

← 10' →

Comparison is with a 4-foot child

TOROSAURUS
TOR-o-SAWR-us

(year named: 1891)

FUN FACTS: The frill is composed of the same kind of bone matter found in human skulls.

LOCATION: Wyoming; South Dakota; Colorado; Utah; New Mexico; Texas; Saskatchewan, Canada

FOOD: Conifers, cycads, ginkgos, flowering plants

SIZE: 36 feet (over 11 m) long, 7 feet (over 2 m) high at the hips

WEIGHT: 4 tons

TRIVIA: The original specimen was collected by John Bell Hatcher, who was nicknamed "the skull finder." He is famous for finding over fifty *Triceratops* skulls in just two summers.

Torosaurus ("pierced lizard") is one of the last of the ceratopsians, or horned dinosaurs. It is best known for one major feature: its frill, which is larger than its skull—which, at 10 feet (3 m), is one of the longest skulls of any land animal in Earth's history. *Torosaurus*'s frill is so long that it severely restricted movement of the skull. The result is that *Torosaurus* would have had to move its whole body, and not just its head, when confronting an attacker. That is why its forelegs were so powerful and highly muscled. Its horns point up and out to the side—directly at the height of an adult *Tyrannosaurus*'s belly.

Torosaurus lived at the same time as *Triceratops*, but the *Torosaurus* population appears to have been much smaller. In *Torosaurus*, the frill is much longer and thinner than in *Triceratops*, and the frill has two fenestrae, or windows, that make it much lighter.

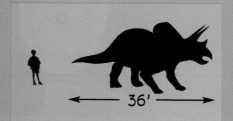

← 36' →

Comparison is with a 4-foot child

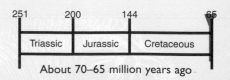

251	200	144	65
Triassic	Jurassic	Cretaceous	

About 70–65 million years ago

TORVOSAURUS
TOR-vo-SAWR-us

(year named: 1979)

Torvosaurus ("savage lizard") is a large meat-eating dinosaur. Its bones are very thick and sturdy, its arms are short but massive, and its thumb claws are huge. It lived in the same environment with several other giant meat-eaters (including *Allosaurus* and *Ceratosaurus*), but *Torvosaurus* was the "bruiser" of the bunch. While *Allosaurus* used its speed and agility to hunt, and *Ceratosaurus* used its oversized teeth, *Torvosaurus* seems to have relied on its brute strength.

Torvosaurus was first found by legendary fossil hunter "Dinosaur" Jim Jensen in the Morrison Formation of Colorado. This formation contains many kinds of plant-eating dinosaurs but is especially known for sauropods, or giant long-necks, like *Apatosaurus, Brachiosaurus,* and *Camarasaurus,* and stegosaurs like *Stegosaurus. Torvosaurus* might have been well suited for attacking young sauropods. It was probably not very fast, but neither were they.

FUN FACTS: The strong arms of *Torvosaurus* are peculiar: The forearms are less than half the length of the upper arm!

LOCATION: Colorado, Wyoming, Utah

FOOD: Sauropods, stegosaurs

SIZE: 33 feet (10 m) long, 8 feet (2.5 m) high at the hips

WEIGHT: 3 tons

TRIVIA: "Dinosaur" Jim Jensen found a giant specimen of *Brachiosaurus* (which he called "*Ultrasaurus*") and a giant specimen of *Diplodocus* (which he called "*Supersaurus*") in the same quarry in which he discovered *Torvosaurus*.

251	200	144	65
Triassic	Jurassic	Cretaceous	

About 154–140 million years ago

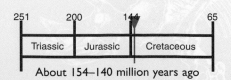

33'

Comparison is with a 4-foot child

125

TRICERATOPS
trie-SAIR-a-tops
(year named: 1889)

FUN FACTS: One scientist assumed the first *Triceratops* specimen belonged to a bison.

LOCATION: Montana, Wyoming, Colorado, South Dakota, Canada

FOOD: Plants

SIZE: Over 33 feet (over 10 m) long, 7 feet (over 2 m) high at the hips

WEIGHT: 5 tons

TRIVIA: In 1999, *Triceratops* became the world's first fully "digital dinosaur." The Smithsonian's complete mounted skeleton—as well as each individual bone—was scanned into a computer and made available on their Web site, where you can move its individual bones. (See Web sites on page 158)

Triceratops ("three-horned face") may hold the record for holding records! It has the largest skull (tied with *Torosaurus* at 10 feet/3 m) and longest hip bone (4 feet/1.2 m) of any dinosaur, the strongest jaw of any land-dwelling herbivore (or plant-eater) that's ever lived, and the largest teeth of any herbivorous dinosaur. It was also the second most famous dinosaur, after *Tyrannosaurus*, for over a century; the first big dinosaur mounted at the Smithsonian Institution; and the first fully restored horned dinosaur (family Ceratopsidae).

With its parrot-like beak, self-sharpening and ever-replacing teeth, massive jaw muscles, 3-foot (1 m) horns, and body more powerful than a rhino, *Triceratops* was the only dinosaur that could (and sometimes did) outfight a *T. rex*!

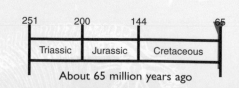

Comparison is with a 4-foot child

33'

251	200	144	65
Triassic	Jurassic	Cretaceous	

About 65 million years ago

TROODON
TRO-o-don
(year named: 1856)

Troodon ("wounding tooth") is a small bird-like theropod. It has very long legs with specialized feet, in which the middle long bone was pinched out at the top to form a shock-absorbing wedge. This allowed it to run very fast. *Troodon* had very large eyes that faced mostly forward, so that it could focus better. It is famous for having one of the largest brains (for its body size) of any dinosaur.

Troodon had a jaw full of many small teeth, but they were not like the teeth of typical meat-eaters. Instead of little serrations running up and down the back of the teeth (as in most meat-eaters), there were much bigger bumps running along the side, as in many plant-eating dinosaurs and lizards. Some paleontologists speculate that *Troodon* may have eaten not only small mammals, lizards, and baby dinosaurs, but also insects, eggs, and even plants.

Paleontologist Dave Varricchio discovered the first *Troodon* nests. Like oviraptorosaurs and ground-dwelling birds, *Troodon* would make a nest on the ground. It would then curl up on top of the nest to brood its eggs.

FUN FACTS: When the first *Troodon* tooth was found, paleontologists thought it was from a lizard!

LOCATION: Montana; Wyoming; Alberta, Canada

FOOD: Possibly small mammals and reptiles, baby dinosaurs, insects, plants

SIZE: 10 feet (3 m) long, 3.1 feet (94 cm) high at the hips

WEIGHT: 110 lbs (50 kg)

TRIVIA: Paleontologist Dale Russell once made a model of what he thought a modern, intelligent, tool-using descendant of *Troodon* would look like. He named this creature a "dinosauroid."

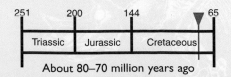

251	200	144	65
Triassic	Jurassic	Cretaceous	

About 80–70 million years ago

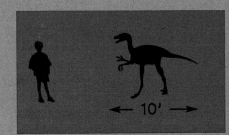

← 10' →

Comparison is with a 4-foot child

127

TYRANNOSAURUS
tie-RAN-o-SAWR-us

(year named: 1920)

Raptor foot

FUN FACTS: A fossilized *T. rex* dropping was found in Saskatchewan, Canada, in 1995. It was filled with the broken and digested bones of a plant-eating dinosaur. The dropping was the size of a loaf of bread!

LOCATION: Montana; Wyoming; South Dakota; Colorado; Texas; New Mexico; Alberta and Saskatchewan, Canada

FOOD: *Anatotitan, Ankylosaurus, Edmontosaurus, Triceratops*

SIZE: 41 feet (12.5 m) long, 13 feet (3.9 m) high at the hips

WEIGHT: 7 tons

FRIENDS: None

ENEMIES: None

TRIVIA: *Tyrannosaurus* had the biggest brain of any dinosaur known.

41'

Comparison is with a 4-foot child

Tyrannosaurus ("tyrant lizard") is one of the most well-known of all dinosaurs. It is no longer considered the largest of the theropods (see *Giganotosaurus*, page 76), but it is certainly one of the fiercest and most powerful. *Tyrannosaurus* is the last and largest of the tyrannosaurs, or tyrant dinosaurs.

Like other tyrant dinosaurs, *Tyrannosaurus* has very short arms with only two fingers. Although these were probably useless while hunting, its jaws were not: *Tyrannosaurus* has an enormous skull armed with teeth the size of bananas! Unlike the teeth of most meat-eaters, tyrant dinosaur teeth are very thick and capable of crushing bones. The skull and neck bones show that *T. rex* had the largest neck muscles of any meat-eating dinosaur. It probably used its strong neck to twist and pull off big chunks of meat that it grasped with its jaws. *Tyrannosaurus* could bite with extremely strong force—one fossilized skeleton shows that it crushed and swallowed the bones of a smaller plant-eating dinosaur.

Most dinosaurs, in general, had eyes facing sideways, which allowed them to see all around themselves. The eyes of *Tyrannosaurus*, though, faced forward so it could focus better on a single object and tell precisely how far away it was.

This would be very useful for a hunter—especially one that had to fight *Triceratops,* one of the most dangerous plant-eating dinosaurs of all.

The legs of the tyrant dinosaurs were long and slender for their size, allowing them to chase down the horned dinosaurs and duckbills that were the most common plant-eaters of their time. In fact, a specimen of the duckbill *Edmontosaurus* shows a bite mark taken out of its tail that matches the bite of *Tyrannosaurus.* Because this bite was healed, we know that the *Edmontosaurus* managed to get away from its attacker!

Although some people think that the female *Tyrannosaurus* was larger than the male, there is no real evidence for this. Indeed, paleontologists do not yet know how to tell a male *Tyrannosaurus* from a female from just the skeleton. It is known, though, that *Tyrannosaurus* led a rough life. Some specimens show many broken bones that had healed over.

TAKE TWO!

In the *Jurassic Park* movies, *Tyrannosaurus* is shown as being a protective parent. While no *T. rex* nest has yet been found, the living relatives of *Tyrannosaurus* (birds and crocodilians) guard their nests and take care of their babies. Similarly, there is evidence from the nests of smaller meat-eaters and from various planteaters that many dinosaurs were good parents. So the simplest explanation at present is that, fearsome though it may have been, *Tyrannosaurus* probably looked after its eggs and young.

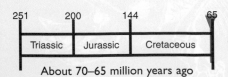

251	200	144	65
Triassic	Jurassic	Cretaceous	

About 70–65 million years ago

129

VELOCIRAPTOR

vuh-LOS-ih-RAP-tor

(year named: 1924)

FUN FACTS: A fossil of *Velociraptor* has been found with a bite mark through the top of the skull. The bite matches that of another *Velociraptor*. This shows that *Velociraptors* killed each other.

LOCATION: Mongolia, China

FOOD: *Protoceratops, Oviraptor, Shuvuuia,* other dinosaurs

SIZE: About 6.6 feet (2 m) long, 1.5 feet (50 cm) high at the hips

WEIGHT: 33 lbs (15 kg)

TRIVIA: In the movie *Jurassic Park*, Dr. Grant is digging up a skeleton of *Velociraptor* in Montana; this would indeed be an amazing discovery, as true *Velociraptor* is known only from Asia!

Velociraptor ("swift hunter") is probably the most famous meat-eating dinosaur after *Tyrannosaurus*. Although it was first described in 1923, it was made famous to most people by its starring role in *Jurassic Park*.

Velociraptor is one of the dromaeosaurs, or raptor dinosaurs. It is actually a pretty small, but fierce, dinosaur, with a skull only 7 inches (18 cm) long. (The dinosaurs shown in *Jurassic Park* are too big to be true *Velociraptors*.) Its arms are long and end in powerful grasping claws. Its feet have huge sickle-shaped claws, which could retract when not in use.

A spectacular fossil from Mongolia shows exactly how these claws were used. The fossil shows a *Velociraptor* and a little horned dinosaur—*Protoceratops*—locked in their final battle. The hands of the *Velociraptor* are clutching the skull of the *Protoceratops,* while the left foot claw of the raptor is buried deep in the horned dinosaur's neck. The *Velociraptor* was apparently in the midst of ripping out the throat of the *Protoceratops* when the two were buried in a

← 6.6' →

Comparison is with a 4-foot child

sand dune. (The little horned dinosaur seems to have had its revenge, however, as the *Velociraptor*'s right arm was in its beak. The *Protoceratops* no doubt bit it off with its final bite!)

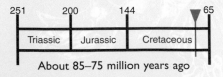

251   200   144   65
Triassic | Jurassic | Cretaceous

About 85–75 million years ago

WUERHOSAURUS

woo-EHR-ho-SAWR-us

(year named: 1994)

FUN FACTS: Stegosaurs were probably the slowest of all dinosaurs. The thighbone is almost twice as long as the shin bone—the opposite of what you'd find in high-speed animals. In *Wuerhosaurus,* we see another dinosaur that gave up any chance at speed to put all of its effort into defense.

LOCATION: Mongolia, China

FOOD: Conifers, cycads, ginkgos

SIZE: 27 feet (8.1 m) long, 6 feet (1.8 m) high at the hips

WEIGHT: 4 tons

TRIVIA: *Stegosaurs,* in general, are the rarest of all the dinosaur groups because not many species evolved.

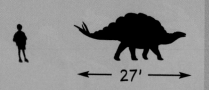

← 27' →

Comparison is with a 4-foot child

Wuerhosaurus ("lizard from Wuerho") is a rare type of stegosaur from the Cretaceous Period. Well before the final extinction of the dinosaurs, stegosaurs became extinct and were replaced by ankylosaurs. The reason this occurred may be found by comparing their features. Although stegosaurs were well covered with plates on their backs and tails, their sides were less protected. Ankylosaurs were fully armored, and this may help explain why stegosaurs became extinct first. The presence of this stegosaur (*Wuerhosaurus*) in China—well into the Cretaceous—suggests that an isolated group survived in that area.

There are two major features that separate *Wuerhosaurus* from a typical *Stegosaurus. Wuerhosaurus* has a shorter body and a wide, flaring hip bone. In stegosaurs in general, the hip bone is so large that it grows up, outward, and over the thighbone.

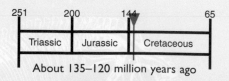

251	200	144	65
Triassic	Jurassic	Cretaceous	

About 135–120 million years ago

ZUNICERATOPS
ZOO-nee-SAIR-a-tops

(year named: 1998)

Z *uniceratops* ("Zuni horned face") was the first ceratopsian, or horned dinosaur, to appear with horns over the eyes (an advanced feature) as well as several primitive features. Also important is the fact that it lived well before most other horned dinosaurs *and* in western North America. For a long time, scientists believed that horned dinosaurs originated in Asia and spread much later to North America. But the discovery of *Zuniceratops*, which was one of the earliest horned dinosaurs, caused scientists to consider another possibility—that ceratopsians arose in North America, later spread to Asia (where new types evolved), and then reentered North America.

Zuniceratops also has single-rooted teeth. (All the later ceratopsians have double-rooted teeth.) This shows that in ceratopsians, the frill and horns evolved first, followed by changes in the teeth.

FUN FACTS: *Zuniceratops* is the only known ceratopsian named after a Native American tribe.
LOCATION: New Mexico
FOOD: Ground cover of cycads, flowering plants
SIZE: 10 feet (3 m) long, 3.3 feet (about 1 m) high at the hips
WEIGHT: 100 pounds (45 kg)
FRIENDS: Hadrosaurs
ENEMIES: Dromaeosaurs
TRIVIA: Teeth of an even earlier ceratopsian, possibly related to *Zuniceratops*, were found in Maryland in 1991.

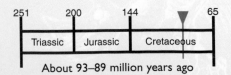

251	200	144	65
Triassic	Jurassic	Cretaceous	

About 93–89 million years ago

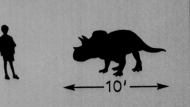

Comparison is with a 4-foot child

←—10'—→

133

The Mesozoic Era is often called the Age of Dinosaurs, but many other types of animals lived at this time. Some of these, such as the insects or the shrew-like early mammals, would not have looked very different from animals today. Others, however, were just as strange and spectacular as the dinosaurs. Following are some of the non-dinosaur reptiles that lived in the Age of Dinosaurs.

MARINE REPTILES

During the Age of Dinosaurs, many groups of reptiles that once had land-living ancestors evolved into swimming reptiles. Most of the groups still spent a lot of time on shore—as do the marine iguanas of the Galápagos Islands today—and had hands and feet that ended in fingers and toes. Others, however, spent almost their whole lives in the water. In these groups, the hands and feet evolved into flippers. Three of the more amazing groups of marine reptiles are plesiosaurs, ichthyosaurs, and mosasaurs.

ELASMOSAURUS
e-LAS-mo-SAWR-us
(year named: 1868)

Elasmosaurus ("plate lizard") is one of the more famous members of the plesiosaurs, or near lizards, a major group of Mesozoic Era marine reptiles. All plesiosaurs had compact bodies with four powerful flippers, which they used to swim through the water. Their tails were generally short, and they may have crawled up onto beaches to lay their eggs, the way sea turtles do today.

Elasmosaurus, like many plesiosaurs, had a small head at the end of a long neck and a mouth full of needle-like teeth. It could swim into schools of fish, moving its head back and forth to catch them. At up to 40 feet (12 m) long, *Elasmosaurus* was among the largest of the long-necked plesiosaurs.

Other plesiosaurs had bodies similar to *Elasmosaurus*'s, but instead of small heads and long necks, they had big heads and short necks! These plesiosaurs had large, conical teeth for catching larger prey. Some of these short-necked plesiosaurs were small, but others grew as big as a sperm whale! These giant plesiosaurs had skulls much bigger than those of the biggest meat-eating dinosaurs, like *Tyrannosaurus*, *Giganotosaurus*, or *Spinosaurus*.

FUN FACTS: When paleontologist Edward Drinker Cope first reconstructed *Elasmosaurus*, he was confused and thought it had a long tail and a short neck!

LOCATION: Kansas

FOOD: Fish

SIZE: 40 feet (12 m) long

WEIGHT: About 4 tons

FRIENDS: None

ENEMIES: *Tylosaurus*

TRIVIA: *Elasmosaurus* had seventy-two neck bones, more than any other animal in Earth's history

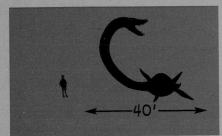

Comparison is with a 4-foot child

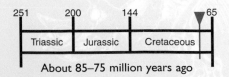

251	200	144	65
Triassic	Jurassic	Cretaceous	

About 85–75 million years ago

OPHTHALMOSAURUS
op-THAL-mo-SAWR-us
(year named: 1874)

Ophthalmosaurus ("eye lizard") was shaped like a dolphin. It had flippers for hands and feet, which it used for steering through the water. It had a dorsal fin on top of its body, and a half-moon-shaped tail fin, which would have helped make it a very fast swimmer.

Ophthalmosaurus was one of the ichthyosaurs, or fish lizards. They were neither fish nor lizards, but were related to the plesiosaurs.

Although dolphins and ichthyosaurs look similar, there are many important differences. Dolphins are a kind of mammal, whereas ichthyosaurs were reptiles. Dolphins primarily use sonar (sending out and listening for special sound waves) to tell where objects are underwater. There is no evidence that ichthyosaurs used sonar, but they did have enormous eyes to see their prey. Ichthyosaurs ate mainly squid and they probably ate some fish.

Ichthyosaurs would not have been able to support themselves on land to lay their eggs. Instead, as fossils show us, their babies grew inside the body of the mother until they were large enough to swim on their own. Then, like dolphins, they were born tail first.

FUN FACTS:
The largest ichthyosaur had eyes over 10 inches (26 cm) across—the largest eyes of any known animal in the history of the Earth!

LOCATION: England

FOOD: Squid and squid-like shellfish, fish

SIZE: 13 feet (4 m) long

WEIGHT: About 2,000 lbs (909 kg)

FRIENDS: None

ENEMIES: Liopleurodon (a giant short-necked plesiosaur)

TRIVIA: Ophthalmosaurus may have been able to dive almost a mile (1.6 km) down in the water while chasing after its food.

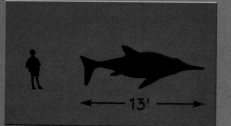

← 13' →

Comparison is with a 4-foot child

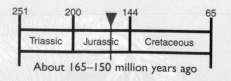

251	200		144	65
Triassic	Jurassic		Cretaceous	

About 165–150 million years ago

TYLOSAURUS

TIE-lo-SAWR-us

(year named: 1872)

Tylosaurus ("knob lizard") has a large, strong chest and arms, big hands, a long body with weak legs, and a strong tail for swimming. It has a ram-shaped snout and big conical teeth for catching prey. It is a mosasaur, or Meuse River lizard, a true marine lizard. The mosasaurs are related to the modern monitor lizards (like the Komodo dragon), Gila monsters, and snakes. Mosasaurs, however, lived their whole lives in the water. As in ichthyosaurs, their young developed inside the mother and were born live into the water.

Mosasaurs were probably not as fast as the earlier ichthyosaurs had been, and instead ambushed their prey the way many sharks do today. Some mosasaurs had flatter teeth than *Tylosaurus*, which they used for cracking open shellfish.

FUN FACTS: A fossil of a giant sea turtle has been found with a flipper bitten off—probably by a *Tylosaurus*.

LOCATION: Kansas, South Africa, Angola, Japan

FOOD: Turtles, plesiosaurs, other mosasaurs, large fish, shellfish

SIZE: 40 feet (12 m) long

WEIGHT: About 5 tons

FRIENDS: None

ENEMIES: None

TRIVIA: Mosasaurs were the first group of extinct reptiles known to science.

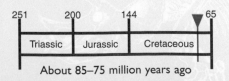

251	200	144	65
Triassic	Jurassic	Cretaceous	

About 85–75 million years ago

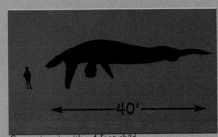

40'

Comparison is with a 4-foot child

137

ARCHOSAURS AND RELATIVES

Archosaurs, or "ruling lizards," is the name given by scientists to a large group of both extinct and modern reptiles. Crocodilians and birds are living archosaurs. Various extinct groups of dinosaurs and pterosaurs are also archosaurs.

Each particular group of archosaurs has its own distinct features. All dinosaurs are archosaurs, but not all archosaurs are dinosaurs. (Remember, to be a dinosaur an animal has to be a descendant of the most recent common ancestor of *Iguanodon* and *Megalosaurus*.) Following are some non-dinosaurian archosaurs that lived during the Age of Dinosaurs, including some extinct crocodilians. Also included is *Tanystropheus,* an archosaur relative.

AETOSAURUS

ay-ET-o-SAWR-us (AY-e-to-SAWR-us)

(year named: 1877)

Aetosaurus ("eagle lizard") was a plant-eater built low to the ground. It had legs that sprawled out to the side and heavy armor protecting its back.

Aetosaurus had a pig-like snout, which it might have used to sniff out tasty plants. Its hands, however, do not seem to have been specialized for digging. The armor on its back was jointed so that it could roll itself up to protect its belly, like a modern armadillo.

During the Late Triassic, the armored dinosaurs had not yet evolved. Perhaps this was because the aetosaurs were already present and there wasn't a place in the environment for a new group of armored plant-eating reptiles.

At the end of the Late Triassic, there was a series of extinctions among the animals and plants on land and in the sea. These extinctions may have been caused by volcanic eruptions, though other factors may have helped. Whatever the cause, aetosaurs (and many other groups) died out at the end of the Late Triassic.

FUN FACTS: Aetosaurs were found in North America, South America, and Europe.

LOCATION: Germany

FOOD: Ferns, cycads

SIZE: 5 feet (1.5 m) long, 1 foot (30 cm) high at the hips

WEIGHT: 100 lbs (45 kg)

TRIVIA: The first aetosaur fossils discovered were of their armor. Because these plates resembled the armor of extinct fish that were found in similar rocks, paleontologists thought they had found a new kind of extinct fish. It wasn't until an aetosaur's bones were discovered that they realized they had found a new kind of reptile.

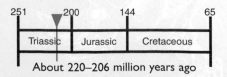

251	200	144	65
Triassic	Jurassic	Cretaceous	

About 220–206 million years ago

← 5' →

Comparison is with a 4-foot child

DEINOSUCHUS
DI-no-SOO-kus

(year named: 1909)

FUN FACTS: Most specimens of *Deinosuchus* consist of individual teeth or armored plates.

LOCATION: Montana, Texas, New Jersey, North Carolina, Georgia, Alabama, Mississippi

FOOD: Large turtles, possibly large fish and dinosaurs

SIZE: 40 feet (12 m) long, about 8 feet (2.4 m) high, maybe more, at the hips

WEIGHT: 9–10 tons

TRIVIA: No modern crocodiles are as big as *Deinosuchus*, but the salt-water crocodile of Australia and the Indian Ocean region grows up to 20 feet (6 m) long, bigger than any land-living predator in the modern world!

Deinosuchus ("terrible crocodile") is a giant crocodilian, closely related to the modern alligators and caimans (Central and South American crocodilians).

Deinosuchus is a gigantic predator up to 40 feet (12 m) long. Because crocodilians are more heavily built than theropods, or meat-eating dinosaurs, the largest *Deinosuchus* would have been larger than the largest *Tyrannosaurus*, *Giganotosaurus*, or *Spinosaurus*.

Deinosuchus is sometimes pictured as eating dinosaurs. While it most likely would have eaten a dinosaur if one came close, it probably hunted prey that was more common in the swamps where it lived. Some paleontologists speculate that it was mostly a hunter of large turtles.

Although crocodilians survived the extinction at the end of the Cretaceous Period, *Deinosuchus* did not.

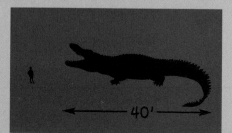

Comparison is with a 4-foot child

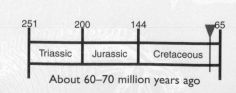

251	200	144	65
Triassic	Jurassic	Cretaceous	

About 60–70 million years ago

LAGOSUCHUS

law-go-SOOK-us

(year named: 1971)

Lagosuchus ("rabbit crocodile") is a little archosaur the size of a rabbit. It had a small, pointed snout, long hind legs, and a long tail.

There were many larger and more interesting creatures living in the Middle Triassic, but Lagosuchus is important to paleontologists for a good reason: It helps us understand where dinosaurs came from.

Lagosuchus had long shins and feet. Its legs were not sprawled out at the side (as in most reptiles) but were held directly underneath the body. This would have allowed it to run fast for a long time. Dinosaurs also have these features. In fact, Lagosuchus seems either to be the ancestor of the dinosaurs or a close relative of that ancestor.

Although we often think of dinosaurs as giant creatures, they didn't start that way. The earliest dinosaurs were small. Having legs directly underneath the body helped early dinosaurs run after insects and small reptiles, and run away from bigger meat-eaters. The same trait helped the later dinosaurs become giants because legs like that could better support their weight.

FUN FACTS: This possible ancestor of the giant dinosaurs was small enough to have been threatened by a cat!

LOCATION: Argentina

FOOD: Insects, possibly small reptiles

SIZE: 19 inches (50 cm) long, 6 inches (15 cm) high at the hips

WEIGHT: 8 ounces (220 g)

FRIENDS: Herbivorous reptiles

ENEMIES: *Rauisuchus*

TRIVIA: Some paleontologists call this archosaur *Marasuchus*, after the mara—a rodent from South America that looks and acts like a rabbit.

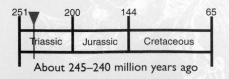

251		200		144		65
	Triassic		Jurassic		Cretaceous	

About 245–240 million years ago

6"

Comparison is with a 4-foot child

141

SIMOSUCHUS

seem-o-SOOK-us

(year named: 2000)

FUN FACTS: When threatened, a *Simosuchus* would probably hunker down so the attacking meat-eater could bite only its tough armor.

LOCATION: Madagascar

FOOD: Ferns, cycads, possibly flowering plants

SIZE: Just over 3 feet (1 m) long, 10 inches (25 cm) high at the hips

WEIGHT: 50 lbs (23 kg)

FRIENDS: None

ENEMIES: None

TRIVIA: Other plant-eating crocodiles are known from the Late Cretaceous of South America.

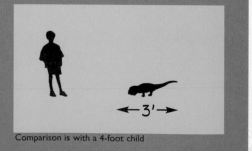

Comparison is with a 4-foot child

Simosuchus ("pug-nosed croco-dile") is a crocodilian—a member of the group that contains living crocodiles, alligators, caimans, gavials, and their extinct relatives—with a short snout. Its teeth are almost identical to those of plant-eating dinosaurs. Its body is covered with heavy armor. In fact, *Simosuchus* seems to be part crocodile, part ankylosaur! This is an example of what paleontologists call "convergent evolution," where two different groups of animals evolve the same basic features because of a similar lifestyle.

People sometimes say that crocodilians are "unchanged since the Age of Dinosaurs." While it is true that some Mesozoic crocodilians look similar to living crocodiles, *Simosuchus* lived on land—in other words, it was not an aquatic predator.

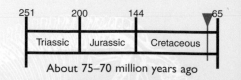

251	200	144	65
Triassic	Jurassic	Cretaceous	

About 75–70 million years ago

TANYSTROPHEUS
tan-ee-STRO-fee-us
(year named: 1852)

Tanystropheus ("long vertebrae") is a strange-looking reptile from the Middle Triassic of Italy. While most animals change shape as they get older, few reptiles changed as much as Tanystropheus!

The main change was in the size of the neck. Baby Tanystropheus had necks shorter than their legs, but adult Tanystropheus had necks longer than the rest of their bodies (head, back, and tail) combined! Although the neck became very long, no neck vertebrae were added. Instead, each vertebra became longer and longer.

Some paleontologists think that Tanystropheus used its long neck to swim into schools of fish and sweep its jaws through them. Others think that the super-long neck was used as a form of display, like the huge tail of a peacock. Both ideas may be correct.

FUN FACTS: The first bones of Tanystropheus found were thought to be part of an early pterosaur.

LOCATION: Italy

FOOD: Fish

SIZE: Over 10 feet (3 m) long, more than 4 feet (1.2 m) high when the neck was raised

WEIGHT: 40 lbs (18 kg); this is only an estimate

FRIENDS: None

ENEMIES: Predatory reptiles

TRIVIA: Before they found complete skeletons, paleontologists thought the neck vertebrae of Tanystropheus were from a dinosaur like Coelophysis.

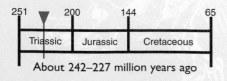

251		200		144		65
	Triassic		Jurassic		Cretaceous	

About 242–227 million years ago

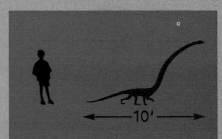

Comparison is with a 4-foot child

143

RAUISUCHUS

ROW-ee-SOO-kus

(year named: 1942)

FUN FACTS: The fossil trackways of *Rauisuchus* and its relatives were first thought to have come from something like a gigantic frog!

LOCATION: Brazil

FOOD: Other reptiles

SIZE: 13 feet (4 m) long, 3 feet (90 cm) high at the hips

WEIGHT: 550 lbs (250 kg)

FRIENDS: None

ENEMIES: None

TRIVIA: Some rauisuchians grew up to 23 feet (7 m) long.

Rauisuchus ("Rau's crocodile"— named after fossil collector Dr. Wilhelm Rau) is one of a group of land-dwelling relatives of the crocodilians called the rauisuchians. These creatures were the top predators on land during the Triassic Period (the beginning of the Age of Dinosaurs).

Rauisuchus and its relatives had heads that looked a lot like those of theropods, or meat-eating dinosaurs. Rauisuchians, however, walked on all fours, while theropods walked on their hind legs. Like a dinosaur's, *Rauisuchus*' legs were directly underneath its body, but unlike a dinosaur, it walked on the soles of its feet. Dinosaurs walked only on their toes, like cats and dogs. Because of this, dinosaurs were probably faster than *Rauisuchus* and its kin.

Rauisuchus lived with the very earliest dinosaurs. It may have hunted these early ancestors of *Tyrannosaurus*, *Velociraptor*, and *Triceratops*.

← 13' →

Comparison is with a 4-foot child

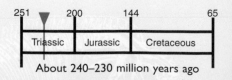

251	200	144	65
Triassic	Jurassic	Cretaceous	

About 240–230 million years ago

PTEROSAURS

Other than the dinosaurs, the most well-known reptiles during the Age of Dinosaurs are probably the pterosaurs ("wing lizards"). Pterosaurs are also archosaurs ("ruling reptiles"), just like the dinosaurs. They are not birds, nor are they any other kind of dinosaur. (Birds are the only known flying dinosaurs.)

Like bats and birds, pterosaurs were flyers rather than gliders. Their arms and hands evolved into wings. They did not have feathers but instead had skin attached to long arms with very long fourth fingers. The other three fingers may have been used for grooming or climbing. The skin in these wings was reinforced inside with slender fibers that made the wings stiffer at the edges.

Pterosaurs had a covering of fur on their bodies, probably to keep them insulated. Although some paleontologists think that pterosaurs walked only on their hind legs, most think they walked something like a gorilla, using their long wings as arms.

Many pterosaurs were small, but some were the largest flying animals of all time. The first pterosaurs appeared in the Late Triassic, around the same time as the first dinosaurs. They died out at the end of the Cretaceous, along with the dinosaurs (except for birds), the marine reptiles, and many other groups of animals. Although it is not certain, the most likely cause for this extinction was the impact of an asteroid with Earth in what is now the Yucatán Peninsula of Mexico. The ash and dust from this explosion would have plunged Earth into darkness and cold, killing off many of the plants that are the base of the food chain both on land and in the sea.

PTERANODON

te-RAN-o-don

(year named: 1876)

FUN FACTS: *Pteranodon* is often shown incorrectly with teeth, or with the tail of a *Rhamphorhynchus*. The *Pteranodon* briefly seen at the end of *The Lost World: Jurassic Park* is shown (correctly) with no teeth, but the *Pteranodon* in *Jurassic Park III* are shown with beakfuls of them (no doubt the result of InGen's genetic manipulations)!

LOCATION: Kansas

FOOD: Fish

WINGSPAN: 26–33 feet (8–10 m)

STANDING HEIGHT: 6 feet (1.8 m)

WEIGHT: 55 lbs (25 kg)

FRIENDS: None

ENEMIES: *Tylosaurus*

TRIVIA: When *Pteranodon* was first discovered, it became very famous. While all the pterosaurs found previously were the size of a seagull or smaller, *Pteranodon* was much bigger than any flying animal today.

*P*teranodon ("wings without teeth") is probably the best known of the more advanced pterosaurs, called pterodactyls ("winged fingers"). There are several species of *Pteranodon*, each with a distinctive crest on the back of the head. All species of *Pteranodon*, however, had long, slender beaks that were totally toothless. They probably ate fish that they caught while skimming over the water.

Pteranodon is known from thousands of fossils, most of which are just broken fragments but some of which are complete skeletons. It had a wingspan of at least 26 feet—possibly 33 feet for the largest specimens—which made it one of the largest of all flying creatures in the history of Earth. For many decades, it was the largest pterosaur known, but larger ones have since been discovered. (*Quetzalcoatlus* had a wingspan of 36 feet/11 m, and *Ornithocheirus* had a wingspan of up to 43 feet/13 m!)

Pteranodon flew above the seas of Kansas during the Late Cretaceous. Although it must have come to land to roost and lay its eggs, it does not appear to have lived much on the mainland. Therefore, pictures showing it flying over the

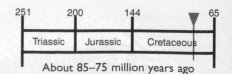

251	200	144		65
Triassic	Jurassic	Cretaceous		

About 85–75 million years ago

heads of tyrant dinosaurs, horned dinosaurs, and/or duckbill dinosaurs are most likely wrong.

33'
(wingspan)

Comparison is with a 4-foot child

147

QUETZALCOATLUS

KET-sal-ko-AHT-lus

(year named: 1975)

FUN FACTS:
The full name of this species, *Quetzalcoatlus northropi,* honors the Northrop Aviation Company, which built a plane called the Flying Wing that looked something like a pterosaur.
LOCATION: Texas; possibly Alberta, Canada
FOOD: Fish, possibly carrion
WINGSPAN: 36 feet (11 m)
STANDING HEIGHT: 11 feet (3.3 m)
WEIGHT: Unknown, maybe only 350 lbs (160 kg)
TRIVIA: *Ornithocheirus,* a pterosaur from the Early Cretaceous of Brazil and Europe, might have been even bigger than *Quetzalcoatlus:* Its wingspan seems to have reached 43 feet (13 m)!

Quetzalcoatlus (after Quetzalcoatl, the "feathered serpent" of Aztec mythology) is one of the biggest animals ever to fly. It is an immense animal, with a head possibly 10 feet (3 m) long in the biggest individuals. It has a wingspan of 36 feet (11 m), and possibly more.

Like *Tapejara* and *Pteranodon,* this giant pterosaur was a pterodactyl (one of the short-tailed pterosaurs). Unlike *Tapejara* and *Pteranodon,* though, *Quetzalcoatlus* lived on the mainland. Although some paleontologists have speculated that it was mostly a carrion-eater (like a vulture), others think that it probably ate mostly fish. It had very long legs, so it could wade into the water like an immense stork.

It lived at the very end of the Age of Dinosaurs, flying over the heads of *Tyrannosaurus, Triceratops,* and *Anatotitan.*

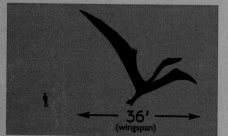

← 36' →
(wingspan)

Comparison is with a 4-foot child

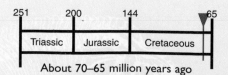

251	200	144	65
Triassic	Jurassic	Cretaceous	

About 70–65 million years ago

RHAMPHORHYNCHUS

RAM-fo-RING-kus

(year named: 1847)

FUN FACTS: Pterosaur bones are even thinner-walled than bird bones.
LOCATION: Germany
FOOD: Fish
WINGSPAN: 5.7 feet (1.75 m)
STANDING HEIGHT: 10 inches (25 cm)
WEIGHT: 1.5 lbs (680 g)
FRIENDS: *Archaeopteryx*
ENEMIES: *Compsognathus*
TRIVIA: Many pterosaur fossils have been found in the same rocks as *Rhamphorhynchus*. Among these is *Pterodactylus*, the first pterosaur ever known (first described in 1784).

Rhamphorhynchus ("beak snout") was a primitive long-tailed pterosaur. From skin impressions, we know that the tip of its tail ended in a diamond-shaped fin. This was probably used for steering.

Rhamphorhynchus lived in the tropical islands of Late Jurassic Europe. It ate fish. From the pointed and upturned shape of its snout, paleontologists think that *Rhamphorhynchus* would fly just above the surface of the water and spear fish with its jaws.

Early pterosaurs rarely got much larger than *Rhamphorhynchus*, although one is known that was probably as big as a bald eagle.

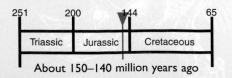

251	200	144	65
Triassic	Jurassic	Cretaceous	

About 150–140 million years ago

5.7' (wingspan)

Comparison is with a 4-foot child

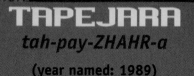

FUN FACTS:

The Santana Formation of Brazil contains the fossils of many different pterosaurs. Each is distinct in its own way: Some of these have tall crests; some have short, heavy beaks; and some (like *Ornithocheirus*) are gigantic.

LOCATION: Brazil
FOOD: Probably fish
WINGSPAN: 26 feet (8 m)
STANDING HEIGHT: 10.5 feet (3.2 m)
WEIGHT: Unknown, estimated at 55 lbs (25 kg)
TRIVIA: Many of the pterosaurs, fish, and even dinosaurs found in the limestones with *Tapejara* have muscle tissue that has petrified, or turned to stone. Unfortunately, because the muscles have turned to stone, they no longer contain DNA.

*T*apejara (after the Tapejara, an ancient being in Tupi Indian mythology) is one of the more advanced kinds of pterosaurs known as a pterodactyl.

Pterodactyls ("winged fingers") generally had shorter tails than primitive pterosaurs. Although some pterodactyls were small, many were eagle-sized or larger. The bones in the palm of a pterodactyl's hand were much longer than the palm bones in primitive pterosaurs, making their wings even longer.

Each species of pterodactyl had its own distinctive crest on its head. Even within each species, there seem to be some individuals that have bigger and better-developed crests than others. Some scientists think that those with the bigger crests were the males and those with the smaller crests were the females. Perhaps the big crests were used for display, like the tails of peacocks.

The crest in some *Tapejara*s is very strange. There is a single spike near the front of the snout that is taller than the skull is long.

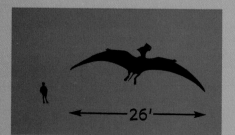

← 26' →

Comparison is with a 4-foot child

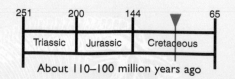

251	200	144	65
Triassic	Jurassic	Cretaceous	

About 110–100 million years ago

Triassic Period

During the Triassic Period, the landmasses of Earth were joined into a supercontinent called Pangaea, which means "all Earth."

Jurassic Period

During the Jurassic Period, Pangaea began to break apart and become separated by water. Notice how North America began to drift away from Africa, forming the very beginnings of the Atlantic Ocean.

Cretaceous Period

During the Cretaceous Period, the continents moved closer to their present-day positions. This separation of landmasses increased the differences among the plants and animals that developed on the different continents.

DINOSAUR DISCOVERIES AROUND THE WORLD

Dinosaur fossils have been found on every continent. Indicated on the map below are over thir
of the most important spots on Earth where dinosaur fossils have been discovered. Some of
these are important for historical reasons, others are more recent sites where new discoveries
are still being made.

(For a more complete listing of sites, see the chapter on
dinosaurian distribution in *The Dinosauria,* edited by
Weishampel, Dodson, and Osmólska.)

Throughout this list, *LT* means Late Triassic; *EJ, MJ,* and *LJ*
are Early, Middle, and Late Jurassic; and *EK* and *LK* are
Early and Late Cretaceous.

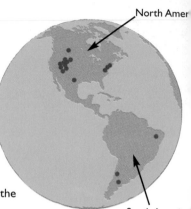

North Amer

South America

North America:

Ghost Ranch, NM *(LT):* A site where hundreds of
  Coelophysis of all ages died and were buried together.
Connecticut River Valley, CT and MA *(LT–EJ):* The first
  dinosaur footprints studied by scientists.
Kayenta Formation, AZ *(EJ):* The rocks of the Kayenta contain the
  best Early Jurassic fossils in North America, including
  Dilophosaurus.
Morrison Formation sites *(LJ):* This real-life "Jurassic Park" is a series of rocks that formed along the
  eastern side of the ancestral Rocky Mountains back in the Late Jurassic. The formation has
  produced more different kinds of dinosaur fossils than any other known to paleontology. Some
  of the most important sites in the Morrison include:
  Como Bluff, WY: One of the best-studied sites. Twenty-six separate quarries here have each
    produced one or more dinosaur fossils.
  Dinosaur National Monument, UT-CO border: Made a National Monument because of the
    completeness of the fossils found here in an old Jurassic riverbed.
  Howe Quarry, WY: Still producing many excellent dinosaur fossils, and has since the 1930s.
  Garden Park, CO: The type (name-holding) specimens of many of the Morrison's dinosaurs come
    from here. Several are on display at the Smithsonian Institution.
  Cleveland-Lloyd Dinosaur Quarry, UT: Over forty *Allosaurus* individuals were found in a single place
    here.
Cloverly Formation, WY-MT border *(EK):* The most complete Early Cretaceous dinosaur fossils
  (including *Deinonychus*) in North America.
Paluxy River, TX *(EK):* An important footprint site that recorded a large meat-eater attacking a giant
  sauropod.
Arundel Clay, MD *(EK):* Has produced fossils of more dinosaur (and other Mesozoic land vertebrate)
  species than any other eastern North American Cretaceous site.
Moreno Hills Formation, NM *(LK):* Newly discovered; contains fossils of the oldest horned dinosaurs
  and therizinosaurs in North America.
Two Medicine Formation, MT *(LK):* Numerous preserved dinosaur nest sites and a bone bed "grave-
  yard" of thousands of individuals of the duckbill dinosaur *Maiasaura.*
Dinosaur Provincial Park, Alberta *(LK):* The most abundant, diverse, and complete Late Cretaceous
  dinosaur fossils.
Haddonfield, NJ *(LK):* Site of the discovery of the duckbill *Hadrosaurus,* the first dinosaur named from
  east of the Misssissippi River.
Hell Creek Formation, MT *(LK):* Contains the geologically youngest fossils of dinosaurs (other than
  birds) in North America, including such famous dinosaurs as *Triceratops, Anatotitan,* and
  Tyrannosaurus.

South America:

Ischigualasto Formation, Argentina *(LT):* The best site for the oldest dinosaurs known to science, including *Eoraptor* and *Herrerasaurus.*

Santana Formation, Brazil *(EK):* Amazingly well preserved fossils that include the remains of dinosaur muscle tissue!

Neuquen, Argentina *(LK):* Formations in these badlands of Patagonia have produced many different species of Late Cretaceous dinosaurs, from babies to adults.

Europe:

Trossingen, Germany *(LT):* Famous for many specimens of *Plateosaurus* and the remains of one of the oldest known turtles.

Stonesfield, England *(MJ): Megalosaurus* (the first dinosaur known to science) was discovered here.

Solnhofen Limestone, Germany *(LJ):* Most famous as the only known site of the early bird *Archaeopteryx.* Has produced many pterosaur fossils, as well as the little theropod *Compsognathus.*

Wealden Group in the UK, especially the Isle of Wight *(EK):* Contains the skeletons of *Iguanodon* and many other Early Cretaceous European dinosaurs.

Bernissart, Belgium *(EK):* The first complete *Iguanodon* skeletons were discovered here.

Las Hoyas, Spain *(FK):* Newly discovered, this site has produced many early bird fossils, as well as the early ostrich dinosaur *Pelecanimimus.*

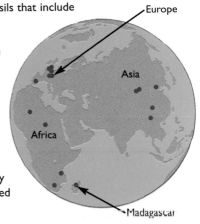

Africa:

Upper Elliot Beds, South Africa, Lesotho, and Zimbabwe *(EJ):* The best Early Jurassic dinosaur skeletons in the Southern Hemisphere.

Tendaguru Hill, Tanzania *(LJ):* Giant sauropods like *Brachiosaurus,* as well as stegosaurs and smaller herbivores, make this Jurassic site famous.

Gadoufaouna, Niger *(EK): Ouranosaurus, Lurdusaurus,* and other large dinosaurs from the middle of the Cretaceous have been found in this Sahara Desert location.

Bahariya Oasis, Egypt *(LK):* Home of *Spinosaurus!*

Maevarano Formation, Madagascar *(LK):* Many new species have been discovered here in the last few years.

Asia:

Lufeng, Yunnan Province, China *(EJ):* The most completely known dinosaur community of the Early Jurassic.

Zigong, Sichuan Province, China *(MJ):* By far the most completely known Middle Jurassic dinosaurs come from Zigong.

Sihetun, Liaoning Province, China *(EK):* Site of the discovery of the amazing feathered dinosaur specimens.

Flaming Cliffs, Ukhaa Tolgod, and Nemegt Valley, Mongolia *(LK):* Three different sites in Mongolia, containing the (sometimes spectacularly preserved) fossils of dinosaurs from the Late Cretaceous of Asia. Home of *Velociraptor* and *Protoceratops!*

Australia:

Muttaburra, Queensland *(EK):* Home of *Muttaburrasaurus.*

Dinosaur Cove, Victoria *(EK):* Famous for fossils of polar dinosaurs!

WHERE TO SEE DINOSAURS IN MUSEUMS

These are some of the biggest museums with dinosaur displays in the United States and Canada.

U.S.A.

CALIFORNIA

Natural History Museum of Los Angeles County
900 Exposition Boulevard
Los Angeles, CA 90007
(213) 763-DINO
www.lam.mus.ca.us
This is the largest museum with dinosaurs in California and has been featured in many films where the action takes place in a museum.

COLORADO

Denver Museum of Nature and Science
2001 Colorado Boulevard
Denver, CO 80205-5798
(303) 322-7009 or (800) 925-2250
www.dmnh.org
This museum has one of the newest dinosaur halls, with excellent displays on ankylosaurs and stegosaurs.

CONNECTICUT

Peabody Museum of Natural History, Yale University
170 Whitney Avenue
New Haven, CT 06520-8118
(203) 432-5050
www.peabody.yale.edu
This is the original dinosaur museum in the U.S. and contains many of the first dinosaurs to be mounted. The Rudolph Zallinger mural *The Age of Reptiles* on the walls of the Great Hall of Dinosaurs is world-renowned.

ILLINOIS

Field Museum of Natural History
1400 South Lake Shore Drive
Chicago, IL 60605-2496
(312) 922-9410
www.fmnh.org
This is the home of "Sue," the *T. rex*. The dinosaur hall is one of the latest to be completely renovated.

MINNESOTA

Science Museum of Minnesota
120 West Kellogg Boulevard
St. Paul, MN 55102
(651) 221-9444
www.sei.mus.mn.us
There are many fine casts and original displays of dinosaurs from the Rocky Mountains here.

MONTANA

Museum of the Rockies
600 West Kagy Boulevard
Bozeman, MT 59717
(406) 994-2251
www.museumofthe rockies.org
This is one of the largest dinosaur museums in the world and has a world-class exhibit on ornithischians.

NEW MEXICO

New Mexico Museum of Natural History and Science
1801 Mountain Road, NW
Albuquerque, NM 87104
(505) 841-2800
www.nmmnh-abq.mus.nm.us/nmmnh/nm mnh.html
This is the largest museum in the New Mexico–Arizona area.

NEW YORK

American Museum of Natural History
Central Park West at 79th Street
New York, NY 10024-5192
(212) 769-5100
www.amnh.org
This is the "crown jewel" of natural history museums. The *two* dinosaur halls contain some of the most famous dinosaurs in the world.

OHIO

Cleveland Museum of Natural History
Wade Oval Drive at University Circle
Cleveland, OH 44106-1767
(216) 231-4600
www.cmnh.org
This is the only place to see *Haplocanthosaurus*.

PENNSYLVANIA

Academy of Natural Sciences
1900 Benjamin Franklin Parkway
Philadelphia, PA 19103
(215) 299-1000
www.acnatsci.org
This is the museum of two legendary dinosaur paleontologists of the 19th century, Joseph Leidy

and Edward Drinker Cope. The newly remodeled dinosaur hall has several unique displays, such as *Avaceratops* and *Hadrosaurus*.

Carnegie Museum of Natural History
4400 Forbes Avenue
Pittsburgh, PA 15213
(412) 622-3131
www.carnegiemuseums. org/cmnh
This is the "home of the sauropods," the only museum where *Apatosaurus* and *Diplodocus* are mounted side by side. The original *T. rex* skeleton is also mounted here.

TEXAS

Dallas Museum of Natural History
3535 Grand Avenue in Fair Park
Dallas, TX 75226
(214) 421-DINO
www.dallasdino.org
This museum has many displays of Cretaceous dinosaurs.

UTAH

Brigham Young University Earth Science Museum
1683 North Canyon Road
Provo, UT 84602
(801) 378-3680
http://cpms.byu.edu/ESM/ index.html
This was the home of "Dinosaur" Jim Jensen, and many of his finds are on display.

Utah Museum of Natural History
1390 East Presidents Circle, University of Utah
Salt Lake City, UT 84112-0050
(801) 581-6927
www.umnh.utah.edu/ home.html
This museum has many Jurassic dinosaurs on display, and another building for paleontology is being added.

WASHINGTON, D.C.

National Museum of Natural History, Smithsonian Institution
10th Street and Constitution Avenue
Washington, DC 20560
(202) 357-2700
www.nmnh.si.edu/paleo/ dino

This the official museu of the United States o America, the home of first mounted skeleton *Triceratops*, *Ceratosaurus* and *Thescelosaurus*, plu the first dinosaur hall t feature all of its exhibit on the Internet.

WISCONSIN

Milwaukee Public Muse
800 West Wells Street
Milwaukee, WI 53233
(414) 278-2702
www.mpm.edu
This museum does acti research in the Cretaceous formations the Rocky Mountains.

CANADA

ALBERTA

Royal Tyrrell Museum o Palaeontology
Four miles northwest o Drumheller, Highway 83
Mailing address:
Box 7500
Drumheller, Alberta
T0J 0Y0
Canada
(403) 823-7707 or (888 440-4240
www.tyrrellmuseum.cor
This is the largest, and best, dinosaur museum i western Canada.

ONTARIO

Canadian Museum of Nature
240 McLeod Street
Ottawa, Ontario K1P 6
Mailing address:
P.O. Box 3443
Station "D"
Ottawa, Ontario K1P 6P
Canada
(613) 566-4700 or (800) 263-4433
www.nature.ca
Their dinosaur hall has the only mounts of *Leptoceratops* and *Brachyceratops* in the world.

Royal Ontario Museum
100 Queen's Park
Toronto, Ontario M5S 2C6
Canada
(416) 586-8000
www.rom.on.ca
This is one of the best museums east of the Mississippi River. It has one of the best displays duckbill dinosaurs in the world.

HERE TO SEE DINOSAURS IN THE FIELD

Places where you can see dinosaurs as they have been found—and are being found—in the rock.

OLORADO

Dinosaur National Monument
4545 East Highway 40
Dinosaur, Colorado 81610-9724
(970) 374-3000
www.nps.gov/dino
For information about the entire area, call the Dinosaurland Travel Board at (800) 477-5558. On exhibit at this monument is a wall (once the bed of an ancient river) where the fossils of many different Jurassic dinosaurs are exposed.

Dinosaur Ridge National Landmark
16381 West Alameda Parkway
Morrison, CO 80465
(303) 697-DINO
www.dinoridge.org
This is one of the best places in the world to see the footprints of Cretaceous ornithopods.

ONNECTICUT

Dinosaur State Park
400 West Street
Rocky Hill, CT 06067-3506
(860) 529-8423
www.dinosaurstatepark.org
The dome of this museum is built directly over the fossilized tracks of Triassic dinosaurs and other reptiles; you can actually see the footsteps of ancient dinosaurs as they are preserved in the rock.

EXAS

Dinosaur Valley State Park
P.O. Box 396
Glen Rose, TX 76043
(254) 897-4588
www.tpwd.state.tx.us/park/dinosaur/dinosaur.htm
This site has footprints of Cretaceous sauropods and theropods in the place where they were discovered.

TAH

Cleveland-Lloyd Dinosaur Quarry
C/o Bureau of Land Management
Price Field Office
125 South 600 West
Price, UT 84501
(435) 636-3600
www.blm.gov/utah/price/quarry.htm
The remains of over forty-four individual *Allosaurus*, as well as other dinosaurs, were collected at this world-famous site.

WYOMING

Red Gulch Dinosaur Tracksite
C/o Bureau of Land Management
Worland Field Office, P.O. Box 119
Worland, WY 82401-0119
(307) 347-5100
www.wy.blm.gov/whatwedo/tracsite.new/rgdt_new.html
This site features thousands of Middle Jurassic theropod footprints.

Wyoming Dinosaur Center
110 Carter Ranch Road
Thermopolis, WY 82443
(307) 864-5522
http://server1.wyodino.org
This museum has daily tours of their excavations in the Jurassic Morrison Formation, where you can see the bones of *Stegosaurus*, *Allosaurus*, and *Diplodocus*.

CANADA

Dinosaur Provincial Park, World Heritage Site
P.O. Box 60
Patricia, Alberta
Canada T0J 2K0
(403) 378-4342
www.gov.ab.ca/env/parks/prov parks/dinosaur
One of the most productive locations for digging dinosaurs is the Dinosaur Park Formation of Alberta, Canada. In the Dinosaur Provincial Park, you can visit sites where herds of horned dinosaurs (and other Late Cretaceous creatures) are being uncovered, prepared, and removed for study.

A complete list of places to see dinosaurs in museums and in the field can be found in these books: *Dinosaur Digs* and *Dino-Trekking* (see Recommended Books About Dinosaurs, page 156).

RECOMMENDED BOOKS ABOUT DINOSAURS

Books for Younger Readers

Brett-Surman, M.K., and T.R. Holtz, Jr. The Greenwich Workshop Press, 1998. *James Gurney—The World of Dinosaurs: A North American Selection.* This is the companion volume to the *World of Dinosaurs* U.S. postage stamp series of 1997. Includes information about each of the dinosaurs and their ancient relatives on the stamps.

Brochu, C.A., J. Long, C. McHenry, J.D. Scanlon, and P. Willis. HarperCollins Books, 2000. *Dinosaurs* (Time-Life Guide). An excellent, up-to-date guide to dinosaurs.

Edgar, B. (editor). Insight Guide Books, 1999. *Dinosaur Digs* (Discovery Travel Adventures). Where to see dinosaur excavations, digs, and exhibits.

Glut, D.F. McFarland & Company, 1999. *Carbon Dates: A Day by Day Almanac of Paleo Anniversaries and Dino Events.* Lists famous events in the history of paleontology. For example: "August 23, 1877—Cope names *Camarasaurus*." "June 13, 1953—The world premiere of the classic dinosaur movie *The Beast from 20,000 Fathoms.*"

Halls, Kelly Milner. John Wiley & Sons, 1995. *Dino-Trekking.* Where to find dinosaurs anywhere on display in North America. Lists all museums and exposition with their addresses, hours of operation, and names of dinosaurs on display.

Holtz, T.R., Jr. Sterling Publishing, 2001. *The Little Giant Book of Dinosaurs.* An examination of dinosaur history and evolution. One of the first books on dinosaur cladistics for kids!

Marshall, C. (editor). Marshall Cavendish Press, 1999. *Dinosaurs of the World,* Volumes 1–11. Contains two- and four-page spreads about dinosaurs, the animals and plants of their world, and principles of evolution, extinction, and fossilization.

McGowan, C. HarperCollins, 1997 and 1999. *Make Your Own Dinosaur out of Chicken Bones: Foolproof Instructions for Budding Paleontologists* and *T-Rex to Go: Build Your Own from Chicken Bones.* These two books show how to use the bones of a modern dinosaur (a roasted or boiled chicken) to construct model skeletons of an *Apatosaurus* and *Tyrannosaurus.* Also include recipes for the chicken meat!

Books for Teachers and Parents

Currie, P.J., and K. Padian (editors). Academic Press, 1997. *Encyclopedia of Dinosaurs*. Hundreds of short entries by dozens of paleontologists on all manner of subjects relating to dinosaurs and their world.

Dingus, L., and T. Rowe. W.H. Freeman and Company, 1997. *The Mistaken Extinction: Dinosaur Evolution and the Origin of Birds*. An excellent review of the different ideas about dinosaur extinction and the origin of birds.

Farlow, J.O., and M.K. Brett-Surman (editors). Indiana University Press, 1997. *The Complete Dinosaur*. Forty-seven experts in paleontology contributed to this award-winning volume, which covers more topics than any other major dinosaur book, including dinosaurs in the public eye (such as movies, comic books, and even stamps).

Glut, D.F. McFarland & Company, 1997. *Dinosaurs: The Encyclopedia*. A massive volume with a photograph or illustration of the original specimen of every dinosaur species, as well as text description of its discovery. A series of supplements updates this book on a regular basis.

Lanzendorf, J. (creator). Academic Press, 2000. *Dinosaur Imagery: The Science of Lost Worlds and Jurassic Art* (The Lanzendorf Collection). Images from the world's largest private collection of dinosaur art, with explanations by leading dinosaur scientists and artists. See Mike Brett-Surman's contribution on pp. 40–42, and Tom Holtz's on pp. 54–56.

Paul, G.S. (editor). St. Martin's Press, 2000. *The Scientific American Book of Dinosaurs: The Best Minds in Paleontology Create a Portrait of the Prehistoric Era*. A collection of classic papers from *Scientific American* as well as brand-new chapters discussing the origin, evolution, history, and extinction of dinosaurs. Written to give the interested public the latest information on the cutting edge of dinosaur research.

Weishampel, D.B., P. Dodson, and H. Osmólska (editors). University of California Press, 1992. *The Dinosauria*. Written by and for paleontologists, this book contains chapters on the anatomy and biology of all the major groups of dinosaurs.

DINOSAUR-RELATED WEB SITES (Beware of case sensitive nodes!)

AMERICAN MUSEUM OF NATURAL HISTORY
www.amnh.org

The AMNH has the largest collection and largest exhibits of dinosaurs and other fossil vertebrates anywhere in the world. This site also has much information about their expeditions to the Gobi Desert in Mongolia.

DINOBASE
www.palaeo.gly.bris.ac.uk/dinobase/dinopage.html

This a compendium site with much information on dinosaurs, such as when they were named and other useful facts.

DINOSAUR ART AND MODELING
www.indyrad.iupui.edu/public/jrafert/dinoart.html

This is a great place to begin to explore the world of dinosaur art and scientific restorations.

DINOSAUR MOVIE HISTORY
www.dinosaur.org/MovieHistory.htm

The best site compiling all the information about dinosaurs in the movies.

DINOSAURIA ON-LINE
www.dinosauria.com

An amateur site. The Omnipedia includes important information on the origins and pronunciations of the names of dinosaurs, pterosaurs, marine reptiles, and other prehistoric reptiles. This site also includes the "Dinosaurs in Science Fiction, Literature, and Fantasy" bibliography at www.dinosauria.com/jdp/misc/fiction.htm.

THE DINOSAURICON
www.dinosaur.umbc.edu/main/index.html

An award-winning amateur site, developed by a former student of Dr. Holtz. It has up-to-date information on dinosaur classification and a gallery of skeletal and life restorations by both professional and amateur artists.

EARTHNET INFO SERVER (ILLINOIS STATE GEOLOGICAL SURVEY)
www.denr1.igis.uiuc.edu/isgsroot/dinos/dinos_home.html

This is one of the best link pages, connecting to other Web sites about all things dinosaurian.

FIELD MUSEUM OF NATURAL HISTORY, CHICAGO
www.fmnh.org

This is the home of "Sue" the *T. rex*. Their exhibits also include *Herrerasaurus*.

FIND-A-DIG
www.enteract.com/~chipagan/find.html

If you want to go on a dinosaur dig, this place lists many expeditions that you can join. (See also the book *Dinosaur Digs*, listed in the book references.)

INTERNET RESOURCE GUIDE FOR ZOOLOGY: DINOSAURS
www.biosis.org.uk/htmls/zrdocs/zoolinfo/grp_dino.htm#i

This is the largest link page about dinosaurs.

JURASSIC PARK™ INSTITUTE
www.jpinstitute.com

A resource for dinosaur learning and fun.

MUSEUM OF PALEONTOLOGY, UNIVERSITY OF CALIFORNIA, BERKELEY
www.ucmp.berkeley.edu/diapsids/dinosaur.html

The University of California's Museum of Paleontology Web site is built to reflect the relationships of different groups of animals, plants, and organisms through time. This page discusses the dinosaurs as a whole, and there are links to other pages that discuss all the major groups of dinosaurs, their anatomy, and their history, plus links to other major museums.

MUSEUM OF THE ROCKIES PALEONTOLOGY DEPARTMENT
www.museum.montana.edu

This is the home of Jack Horner, who was the inspiration for Alan Grant in the *Jurassic Park* movies. The Museum of the Rockies' exhibits are more extensive than those of museums in major cities.

NATURAL HISTORY MUSEUM, LONDON
www.nhm.ac.uk

One of the oldest and grandest natural history museums in the world, the Natural History Museum is still a center of dinosaur research. The Dino Directory (http://flood.nhm.ac.uk/cgi-bin/dino) is a new interactive site with basic information and reconstructions of over one hundred different dinosaur genera.

OCEANS OF KANSAS PALEONTOLOGY
www.oceansofkansas.com

Great information about the varied marine life of the Late Cretaceous. See the marine reptiles, fish, and shellfish that swam Cretaceous seas where Kansas is now!

THE PALAEONTOLOGICAL ASSOCIATION
www.ucmp.berkeley.edu/Paleonet/PalAss/index.html

This is a great society for all kinds of paleontology, including fossil plants and invertebrates. Many professionals subscribe to their e-newsletter.

PEABODY MUSEUM OF NATURAL HISTORY, YALE UNIVERSITY
www.peabody.yale.edu

The Peabody Museum was where many critical discoveries in dinosaur paleontology were made in the 19th and 20th centuries. Make sure you visit the Web page about the famous mural *The Age of Reptiles* by Rudolph Zallinger.

ROYAL TYRRELL MUSEUM OF PALAEONTOLOGY
www.tyrrellmuseum.com

The home page of western Canada's most important museum, featuring a tour of the RTMP's exhibits as well as updates from field expeditions in Canada, Argentina, and elsewhere.

SMITHSONIAN INSTITUTION NATIONAL MUSEUM OF NATURAL HISTORY
www.nmnh.si.edu/paleo/dino

This is the first museum to have a "virtual tour" of their entire dinosaur hall—and the home of the first fully "digital" *Triceratops*.

SOCIETY OF VERTEBRATE PALEONTOLOGY
www.vertpaleo.org

The home page for the premier professional organization of dinosaur scientists and their colleagues in vertebrate paleontology. Provides information about upcoming technical conferences, journals, FAQ's, schools, and so forth.

SO YOU WANT TO BE A PALEONTOLOGIST?
www.cisab.indiana.edu/~mrowe/dinosaur-FAQ.html

This is an FAQ answer list about how to start your career in vertebrate paleontology.

THE TREE OF LIFE PROJECT: DINOSAURIA
www.phylogeny.arizona.edu/tree/eukaryotes/animals/chordata/dinosauria/dinosauria.html

An international multi-year project to map out the entire "Tree of Life," with detailed information on all organisms, past and present. This link is to the dinosaur part of the Tree.

GLOSSARY

Angiosperm ("covered seed"):
A group of seed plants in which the seed is surrounded by a fruit; the flowering plants.

Ankylosaur ("fused lizard"):
Any short-legged, plant-eating dinosaur that is armored with thick, bony scutes (small plates).

Archosaurs ("ruling lizards"):
A group of advanced reptiles including the dinosaurs, pterosaurs, and crocodilians.

Carnivore ("flesh-eater"):
Any meat-eating animal.

Ceratopsian ("horned face"):
A plant-eating dinosaur with horns on its face and a bony frill over its neck.

Cladistics:
A method of classifying organisms in which hypotheses about evolutionary relationships are the basis for classification. Organisms are grouped according to their common ancestors, determined by the identification of shared derived characteristics. Higher groups are not ranked. This system has replaced the older Linnaean system of classification.

Cretaceous ("chalk age"):
The third geological period in the Age of Dinosaurs, from 144 to 65 million years ago.

Crocodilian:
The group of archosaurs including crocodiles, alligators, and gavials.

Dinosaur ("fearfully great lizard"):
Any descendant of the most recent common ancestor of *Iguanodon* and *Megalosaurus*. This group the Saurischia and the Ornithischia.

Dromaeosaurs ("swift-running lizards"—the "raptors"):
A group of advanced theropods with very stiff tails and a sickle-like claw on the second toe of the foot.

Era:
A division of geological time composed of geological periods. The Mesozoic Era includes the Triassic, Jurassic, and Cretaceous Periods.

Evolution ("unfolding"):
The development of plants and animals through geological time, and the way that this development has come about. This is oversimplified in many books as "change over time."

Extinction ("wiping out"):
The death of a group of plants or animals.

Formation:
A formally defined, mappable rock unit.

Fossil ("dug up"):
The remains of something that once lived. Fossils are often millions of years old and have usually turned to stone over time. It is also defined as "evidence of life in the geologic past."

Gastrolith ("stomach stone"):
A pebble or stone that is swallowed by an animal and kept in the digestive tract. Gastroliths grind up food, making it easier to digest.

Geologic time:
1) The period of time from the formation of Earth to the beginning of recorded history; prehistoric time. 2) A very long span of time extending over millions of years.

Gondwana:
The supercontinent or landmass that fragmented millions of years ago to form modern South America, Africa, Antarctica, Madagascar, India, and Australia.

Hadrosaur ("sturdy lizard"):
A group of plant-eating dinosaurs of the Late Cretaceous. Hadrosaurs are often known as "duckbilled dinosaurs" because of their broad, flat snouts.

Herbivore ("plant-eater"):
An organism whose diet consists exclusively or mainly of plants.

Jurassic (from the Jura Mountains, where rocks from this period were first named):
The second geological period in the Age of Dinosaurs, from 200 to 144 million years ago.

Laurasia:
The supercontinent or landmass that fragmented millions of years ago to form modern North America, Greenland, Europe, and Asia.

Linnaean taxonomy:
The older system of classifying life based on a hierarchical system. This includes the ranked categories such as Kingdom, Phylum, Class, Order, and Family. Paleontologists now use Cladistics (see above).

Mesozoic ("middle age"):
The Age of Dinosaurs, the time from 251 to 65 million years ago, which includes the Triassic, Jurassic, and Cretaceous Periods. The Mesozoic Era is the "middle age" between the Paleozoic and Cenozoic Eras.

Omnivore ("all-eater"):
An animal that eats both other animals and plants.

Ornithopod ("bird-foot"):
A plant-eating dinosaur that has no spines or horns and walks on two legs.

Pachycephalosaur ("thick-headed lizard"):
A plant-eating dinosaur with a very thick skull roof, possibly used for head- or flank-butting.

Paleontologist ("expert on ancient life"):
A scientist who studies fossils and the history of life on Earth.

Pangaea ("all Earth"):
A giant ancient supercontinent, made up of all the land area of Earth, which formed during the late Paleozoic Era and later divided into the supercontinents of Laurasia and Gondwana, from which the present continents derived. We now know of at least two earlier supercontinents.

Period:
A division of geological time smaller than an Era, such as the Jurassic, Triassic, or Cretaceous.

Predator:
An animal that hunts and seizes other animals for food.

Prey:
An animal hunted or seized for food; victim of a predator.

Protofeathers:
The ancestral form of the feathers of modern birds; simple tubes found covering the bodies of many advanced theropods.

Sauropod ("lizard-foot"):
A large plant-eating dinosaur with a long neck and a long tail, such as *Diplodocus* or *Apatosaurus*. Lived in the Jurassic or Cretaceous Periods. (Note: A new discovery shows a sauropod in Thailand from the very end of the Triassic.)

Sexual dimorphism:
The occurrence of two distinct male and female forms of the same species, especially visible differences in coloration, body shape, size, and so on.

Species:
A group of organisms that can breed with one another and produce fertile offspring.

Theropod ("beast-foot"):
A group of two-legged, primarily meat-eating, dinosaurs.

Titanosaur:
A group of advanced sauropods of the Late Jurassic and Cretaceous, including some very large forms. Some titanosaurs were armored.

Triassic ("three parts"):
The first geological period in the Age of Dinosaurs, from 251 to 200 million years ago.

Troodonts:
A group of advanced bird-like theropods with large brains and very long, slender legs.

Type specimen:
The original specimen that is designated as the first example, and "name bearer," of a given species or other group of organisms, and that is used as the basis for describing the group; the actual individual specimen first used to name a new species.

ABOUT THE AUTHORS

Realizing he could not grow up to be a dinosaur, **Dr. Thomas R. Holtz, Jr.** did the next best thing and became a vertebrate paleontologist. His specialty is *Tyrannosaurus rex,* and his work on carnivorous dinosaurs has become the standard in several textbooks. In addition to his many scientific papers, he has been involved in the making of several documentaries, including the award-winning *Walking with Dinosaurs* and *When Dinosaurs Roamed America* for The Discovery Channel. Dr. Holtz is a lecturer in the Department of Geology at the University of Maryland, College Park. To learn more about him, visit his Web site at www.geol.umd.edu/~tholtz/tholtz.htm.

As a child, **Dr. Michael Brett-Surman** was deeply affected by seeing the skeleton of *Tyrannosaurus rex* at the American Museum of Natural History. He was so affected, in fact, that he went on to name three new dinosaurs for science: *Secernosaurus, Gilmoreosaurus,* and *Anatotitan*—plus the Mesozoic bird *Avisaurus archibaldi*! Dr. Brett-Surman is the Museum Specialist for Dinosaurs at the National Museum of Natural History of the Smithsonian Institution and a professor in the Geology Department at George Washington University. He was co-editor of the award-winning book *The Complete Dinosaur.*

ABOUT THE ILLUSTRATOR

Inspired by Rudolph Zallinger's mural "The Age of Reptiles," young **Robert Walters** started drawing dinosaurs—and never stopped. He went on to study art at the Academy of the Fine Arts in Philadelphia and has been a professional dinosaur life restoration artist for more than twenty years. His work is on permanent display at museums across the country, including the Smithsonian Institution and the Academy of Natural Sciences. He has illustrated more than twenty dinosaur books and countless magazine articles and has worked on documentaries for PBS and The Discovery Channel. You can visit him on-line at www.dinoart.com.